HOW TO MIND YOUR MIND

Simple Strategies That Have A Powerful Impact
On Your Peace Of Mind, Habits, And Relationships

Colm O'Reilly

HOW TO MIND YOUR MIND

Simple Strategies That Have A Powerful Impact

On Your Peace Of Mind, Habits, And Relationships

Colm O'Reilly

First Edition

Cover & Interior Design: www.JohnEdgar.Design

To Derek, anyone who's lucky enough to know him knows why.

PANDAPUP

COLM O'REILLY
AUTHOR

Colm used to be a stressed mess, and always struggled to achieve what he wanted, or enjoy the good times when they came along. After being referred to suicide counselling for a second time in a row, he committed to finding what really worked when it came to effective, and practical, mental well-being.

Now, he gets to help others implement the skills that helped him build his inner peace - which has helped him build the outer success he was looking for. He owns a CrossFit gym, mentors other owners, is an enthusiastic amateur cyclist and doggo dad.

IG: @oreillycolm

Ph: +353 86 8151092

Email: oreilly.colm@gmail.com

www.thementalhealthplan.com

TABLE OF CONTENTS

My Story / Introduction 1

What Is Mindset Anyway? 5

Your Mindful Minute 29

Compassion & Self Empathy 51

Free Yourself With Forgiveness 77

Happiness Boosters—Gratitude, Savouring, & Kindness 89

We Need To Talk (About How You Talk to Yourself) 103

Fixing Your True North — Identity, Values & Priorities 121

Habits 135

Sustainable Communication 151

Going Deep 167

Enough 175

MY STORY / INTRODUCTION

Splash . . .

There I was, soaking wet and drifting along the Seine River in Paris, having jumped off a bridge, aged seventeen, in an attempt to end my life. I thought I'd die instantly, and that would be better for everyone. It would end the burden I was being in everyone's life and end the feeling of badness inside me. Or at least that's what I thought.

I hit the water, thought "Is this what it's like to be dead?" and then resurfaced a few seconds later and began to drift under the bridge. I'd forgotten I knew how to swim and had thought the second I'd hit the water that would be the end of my suffering.

After a few minutes of forcing myself to take on water (with no success there either) I swam to shore and hoped that death would take me from hypothermia or something. Eventually, after a few minutes or a few hours—I can't remember—I got up and sought help.

I'd like to say that was just a glitch, but I never dealt with what had driven me to take that drastic action. I pushed it down and down and tried to ignore it. Tried to just forget about it and move on. But the suicide attempt was a symptom of a bad life strategy: always attempting to find an external solution to an internal problem.

Throughout my twenties I worked damn hard to prove myself in order to reach the peace of mind I so desperately craved. My internal state always was dictated by what went on in my external world. If I could just get this job, this promotion, win this game, get their approval . . . THEN I'd finally feel at peace with myself. I didn't quite have the language skills or understanding, but if I did, that's what my inner monologue would have sounded like.

I wanted so badly to be approved by others in the form of financial success, relationships, likes, kudos, or just a compliment on my clothes. But deep down, I *knew* I was pathetic. When I say "I knew," I mean that's what I believed—the story was so ingrained in my mind I accepted it as an indisputable truth.

So, I got tossed around by the ups and downs of life—foreboding joy when things were going well and confirming depression when things went south. "You deserve this; you're a fool for believing you deserved to be happy," was how my inner critic liked to speak to me. My internal state—how I felt inside—was always at the mercy of life's events.

Eventually, this all came to a head when a combination of betrayal by a lover and a business partner sent me over the edge again. I was referred back to suicide counselling with Pieta House right as I was launching a new business. That was a dicey few months!

So, when I graduated from Pieta House, I thought, "I simply can't wait around for the next major bout of anxiety and depression to strike." It was unfair on me and unfair on those who count on me—especially my new business partner, who'd taken a chance on us with our fresh new venture. Something had to change. I started looking into what worked and what didn't when it came to mental health and self-care. I treated myself as an N=1 study and started testing different approaches to measure their impact. Did meditation really work? Positive thinking? NLP? What styles of mental self-care are best suited to what person in what circumstance? And what does 'work' even mean anyway? What was the end point?

Slowly, slowly, I found myself less reliant on external circumstances for my mood and less battered by the ups and downs of life. A surprising result was that the external goals I'd so desperately chased started to materialise with less stress and more ease.

Was it perfect? Hell no. There was a lot of two steps forward, ten steps back during that time. I'd gain inner control and then something external would knock me back. I'd try something only to be impatient with results or the magnitude of the impact. But, as I practiced self-care, keeping what worked, and discarding what didn't, my baseline peace of mind definitely improved.

Then, in a bar during a business conference a few years ago, I heard the guys talk about how business owners had much higher rates of anxiety, depression, substance dependency, and suicide. It clicked! I could help people with this! I'd been there before and knew what needed to be done to get to a place where you can not only show up in the world as your best self but also be less impacted by the ups and downs of life!

I first had to formalise my practice into easy-to-understand, actionable steps, but once I did that and started helping others, I realized just how powerful the simple, repeated actions in this book are for taking care of your mind and inner world!

WHY AM I TELLING YOU THIS?

Simply, I want you to know I know what it's like to be down that dark hole, to wish you felt better, to be angry, afraid, hate every minute of your life and hate every part of yourself. And maybe you're there now. Maybe you're nowhere near that, and you're thinking, "Hey, I don't have it that bad at all." That's cool too.

Whether you're at rock bottom or just off form, I want you to know that I know what it's like to not feel good inside your head and that there are steps you can take that will make a real difference.

I'm not a fan of what I'll call "Mindset Escapism"—that's when you use inner work to escape the difficult decisions and actions out in the real world. It's meditating but not changing anything in your life; it's going on long retreats but still being an asshole at work; practicing yoga but not paying off your credit card bill.

In order for Mindset work to be truly effective, it needs to be simple to understand, easy to implement, fit into your day, and impact your life outside your head and "off the cushion." Let's face it, if we can't see change in our lives, we're eventually going to drop our inner self-care. That's the crux of this book: Make it integrated into who you are and what you do daily, with real, tangible results.

I've mentioned the internal and the external, so let's define those terms. **Internal** is our thoughts, feelings, and everything going on inside of us. Our **external** then is our habits, relationships, and environment—which includes where we live, our commute, work, and the society we live in.

Everyone says you should take care of yourself and your mental well-being, but no one tells you exactly how. No one explicitly told me how either. It's a super-valuable skill that we can all benefit from (and I'd argue others benefit from it, too, even if they're not practicing themselves). This book is the step-by-step how-to—but you got that from the title already!

WHAT IS MINDSET ANYWAY?
AND WHY DO WE FIND IT SO HARD TO WORK ON OUR MINDS?

What do we mean by Mindset? Mindset gets thrown around as if it's one specific thing—e.g., "You just need to get into the right mindset"—as if there's a Mindset switch you can just flip and you're there. **Mindset really is how we take care of our thoughts and emotions**. Notice I said "take care," not repress, manipulate, or coerce. Attempts to restrain our darker/more shameful impulses, or force motivation and discipline do not work—I mean, hell, you've already tried that, haven't you? Let's get it out of the way now. You can't suppress emotions; you can't shut your thoughts off. Attempting to do so only leads to bad outcomes. But you absolutely can befriend them (yes, even the scary thoughts) and co-opt them for the easing of suffering and the building of happiness.

Mindset has many facets, like fitness or nutrition. We can make it as simple or as complex as we'd like. **The simplest definition is clarity and compassion in our thoughts, feelings, and our actions.** Minding ourselves, making sure we're at our best so we can do our best for ourselves and everyone else. Knowing this, we can understand that our mindset and our mental well-being is within our sphere of responsibility. Not only can we improve it, but we have an obligation to do so.

This book focuses on the foundations of Mindset—building a healthy relationship with your mind. You can't build any sustainable performance on ill health, so this is where we'll focus first.

THE BABY BRAIN & THE EXTERNAL BIAS

As a baby, you are 100% dependent on the people around you to take care of all your needs. They feed you, clothe you, and protect you from the elements. As you grow, they help you learn to walk, speak, and make sense of the world. Before you know it, your brain has reasoned, "If I have a need, something or someone outside of me is responsible for its fulfilment."

We grow up, and we become more "self-reliant" and "independent" over the years. But without becoming fully conscious of how much we make others or something outside ourselves ultimately responsible. We learn to ask, coerce, or demand things. And when we get truly upset and emotionally heightened, we revert back to that crying baby. None of this is to judge you but to liberate you from this cycle of demand and blame most people are caught up in. As Sean said in *Good Will Hunting*, "It's not your fault."

Society reinforces this with the idea that happiness and fulfilment are on the other side of achievement or at the completion of a task. When you get to school, then you'll be happy. When you get past elementary school, when you get to college, when you graduate, when you get a job, when you find someone, when you get married, when the kids finally come along, when they get to school age, when you finally finish your book, Colm . . .

Now, none of this is malicious; no one sat down one day and said, "Hey, this is how we'll keep people trapped in this unhealthy and unhelpful cycle." Philsopher, neuroscientist and creator of the "Waking Up" meditation app Sam Harris calls this a "cultural blindspot," so just to be different we'll call it a "societal blind spot."

I'm not saying we don't need something to strive for. If we were perfectly fulfilled, we'd stop doing anything and very quickly die out. So, we need a little bit of unfulfillment and incompleteness. A little bit. Without taking care of your inner self and instead allowing this unfulfillment to take over, you can spend your entire life driven by fears you aren't aware of and don't understand, toward goals that are ill defined, and not reaping the rewards of happiness you believed you'd eventually achieve.

Done right, Mindset training fits perfectly into your daily life and doesn't stop you from chasing your goals but rather makes them more enjoyable (or at least makes the struggle more tolerable and meaningful). My aim is to create a virtuous cycle of inner work supporting your outer world, and your outer work improving your inner world. We all have struggles, but you don't need to suffer while struggling. There's a key difference there in the amount and intensity of mental anguish you need to endure.

If 2020 taught us anything, it's that things, people, events, and structures outside of us aren't reliable. They can be taken away due to forces beyond our control. If you lived for holidays, you suddenly couldn't travel or even gather locally. Even if you could, what would be open? If going to the gym, the pub, the cinema, etc. was how you felt good, that was severely curtailed as well. While Zoom is helpful for keeping in touch, we all know it's not the same as face-to-face connection, and so our need for social interaction was dented by the first pandemic year as well.

I'm not saying that any of these things—things, people, events, structures—are bad. In fact, a lot of them are part of a healthy, fulfilling life. It's just that we need something inside of us to get these needs met if we can't take care of them through external means. Relying solely on external factors always puts us at the whims of fate. It's the difference between being tossed around by the ups and downs of life and riding the highs and lows.

To look at the idea that external success and possessions will fix your inner world, try this quick thought experiment. Imagine someone you know who has something you currently lack and want. Do they have the car you want, the job you're after, the job security, time, freedom, body, Instagram followers, relationship, kids, house, clothes, TV, dog, title, connections, etc.? Are they as happy as you think they should be now they've gotten it? Probably not.

The next argument our brains tend to come up with when we hear this is, "But they don't appreciate it; if I gotten it/them, I'd know how to appreciate it/them." Okay then, ask yourself, have you anything that someone else has told you they're jealous or envious of and you've told them it's not all it's cracked up to be? Even reading this book is proof. There are people who would love to have the time to read, the courage to look at their inner world, the intelligence to comprehend it, the safety to sit and read, the ability to understand English, and so on.

The argument for why you don't appreciate what you have is that, while it's good, it's not enough. We'll eventually get to this, but for now, consider what it would be like having a billion dollars. I think we can all agree that having a billion guarantees financial security. If you're reading this, you most likely live in a relatively safe society, you're not under constant threat of attack from a warring village, and the risk of a violent encounter is also relatively low. So, our need for security is generally centred on financial safety. Yet there are billionaires out there who still act fearfully. This is proof enough that having a billion dollars alone isn't enough to provide security. There needs to be more than just the external aspect.

Look at the person you're coveting—are you focusing purely on that one aspect, without taking into account their entire life? Yes, they might have a nice car, but they work till 11:30 p.m. every evening. Or they've a great body but they earn a pittance. Part of this is not seeing the whole picture of someone's life. We'll talk about how the inner critic uses this selective viewpoint later on.

Finally, think of the last time you thought, "I just need to get through this," or "Once I get that, then my stress will be lower," and notice that your stress most likely just transferred onto the next threat. Or look at our lives and what we have that others may want. Are we as happy and as stress-free now that we've gotten that new shiny thing or gotten past that rough patch in our lives? Probably not. Again, I'm not saying that external events don't play a role in our mental well-being—they absolutely do. It's that we cannot *rely* on them *alone* and need to work on our internal state as well.

Now that I've explained why Mindset is important and why you can't rely solely on the outside world to get all your needs met, let's start tackling some of the other objections we'll have.

IT DOESN'T WORK (WRONG STYLE/EXPECTATIONS)

I've heard people say they've tried meditating and it doesn't work—and in their experience, they're probably right. For two reasons:

They didn't have the right style. Some people love lifting weights, others prefer long distance running. Some prefer playing sports, or gentler exercise like yoga. There are different forms of exercise that work for everyone. We all agree, though, that the human body needs daily(-ish) movement to be healthy. No one would swing a golf club and then declare all physical movement is not for them, would they? This is true with the methods of taking care of your mental health. I'll give you the broad, basic brushstrokes in this book for minding your mind, and then you can tweak and adapt them to suit your needs.

Their expectations were too high. Chances are, you've been promised near-immediate, Zenlike clarity and bliss by pausing to use an app for ten minutes. This promise is completely unfair—it's like the lotto ticket grift. You wouldn't go from crippling debt to unlimited riches just because you finally look at your bank account and start budgeting your money. As someone who used to be terrible with money, when I started using a budget app, it took a few months just to understand where my money was going, another few to find out how much I could devote to fun and how much I could put into savings, and another year or so before my net worth was positive. The same is true with taking care of your mind.

So, what are reasonable expectations? It's semi-subjective. If you do one sit-up, you won't have abs. Skip the chips, and you don't drop a percentage point of body fat. But you do feel better that you've done something beneficial for yourself.

What happens over time is increased clarity of thought. Initially, you'll notice just how unclear your thoughts are. This is actually progress, as you're now aware of how unclear you've been inside your head, how conflicted your beliefs and actions have been, and how unconscious you've been for so long on so many things. It's at this stage of awareness that we're tempted to give up once we see how much work it might be to untangle all the mess in our heads. It might seem like an impossible task. This is why compassion is so important to reassure and guide ourselves like we would a child learning how to ride a bike. Once you're aware, you can begin the process of change (or not; whatever is the right thing for you).

With increased clarity, you'll begin to be able to untangle and disengage from certain events, people, thoughts, and beliefs. You'll see what *their* issues are and what *your* issues are. You'll see what's their issues, and what's your issues. You'll see if you're really angry about the traffic or angry about your life. You'll see how wrapped up and blended, personal and unfair the unconscious automatic mind makes everything.

And the more you notice this, the more you'll go from **reactivity** (impulsively acting our of habit)to **responsiveness** (deliberate, conscious and compassionate actions). You'll be in a better position to choose your response, internal and external, to what happens in the world. Now, you won't be able to do this at the most triggering events and with the most heightened emotions, but you will be less likely to get upset when the barista is slow or your living room is slightly messy. The more you commit to taking care of your inner mind through some focused self-care, the better you'll be able to deal with the stress of a job, a fight with a spouse, or Munster losing yet another final to Leinster.

Ultimately, you'll increase your peace of mind. How happy, calm, and okay you are will be determined less and less by what's going on outside of you. Note that I didn't give an absolute there. Outside factors play a role.

I'm not for one second pretending they don't. Right now, as I write this, I'm tired from a restless night with a sick dog, and despite my nap, my focus isn't one hundred percent But, it's also warm and sunny, so that's beneficial. With greater understanding of our mind, and how it filters what goes on, we can become semi-permeable. This means we are better able to let the good in, without the bad impacting us as much.

At the same time that you're less affected by the outside world, you'll become less affected by your inner world. Naval Ravikant, US Investor who's more known for his insightful tweets on health and happiness, calls this "peace from mind," i.e., you're no longer tormented by your thoughts. You don't react to them as true statements but rather simply thoughts that you can accept, reject, or investigate.

That's the long-term benefit of meditation or deliberate Mindset work. The immediate benefit is feeling good that you did something healthy for your mind—that virtuous feeling like eating a salad or saying no to an unnecessary purchase.

If the result of working on your mind is peace, the opposite we'll define as stress, which leads us to our next common objection.

YEAH, BUT I REALLY DO HAVE PROBLEMS THAT THINKING WON'T SOLVE

In my work with clients, the first objection they'll have is that their stress isn't a result of their thoughts, beliefs, or feelings, but something tangible outside of them. Something "real." This can be salary stress, work stress, relationship stress (or lack thereof), debt stress, misbehaving-kid(s) stress, car-trouble stress, tax stress, holiday stress, travel stress, etc.

This is a result of what we learnetin childhood, as explained above. If people and circumstances outside of us are responsible for meeting our needs, they're also responsible for what we feel. If the outside world solves my problems, it also causes my problems. This is very ingrained in our psyche and will often show up in situations where we lack any sense of control.

We can dismantle this objection pretty easily when we start to see that two people in the same situation, or yourself facing the same outside dilemma at different times, will have different responses to it. Some may find their work week exhausting, whereas for another it's exhilarating. Some people will feel insecure any time their bank balance is less than $100, but for others it's $1,000 or even $10,000. And for others, they're perfectly okay being in the red.

It's clear that our mental filters and our thoughts about our situation have more of an influence on our mental well-being than our circumstances. Of course, there are a few caveats. Let me be clear that if you're homeless and facing a knife-wielding assailant bent on killing you, then yes, you need to focus on external fixes and not count deep breaths in the lotus position!

Mindset work is part of your complete health and key to a full life. Health isn't even enough. If you had perfect physical and mental health, without companionship and meaning it wouldn't be considered a fulfilling life by anyone. Believing that stress will disappear once your stressors go away (spoiler alert: stressors are never going away), or that happiness can only be the byproduct of achieving some physical goal, ignores the impact our mindset has on our well-being.

OTHER PEOPLE NEED THIS, NOT ME

Okay, you understand Mindset is important and can think of someone in your life who could definitely benefit from it. If they only saw their destructive beliefs and patterns, and made some simple changes, then they'd have it so much better! Guess what? People see *your* destructive habits and beliefs and think that *you* could benefit from some simple shifts in perspective and attitude! When we work on ourselves, we develop the ability to step back and see ourselves more clearly. We can develop the ability to look at ourselves more objectively, look at how we're interpreting life and interacting with the world, and what habits are healthy versus harmful.

The urge to change people is strong. Part of this can be explained by my good friend Walter, when he said, "It's so difficult to change ourselves that we spend all of our time trying to change other people—which is impossible!"

Claiming that "others need this" can also be a defence mechanism. You're afraid that by admitting your faults you'll be less than acceptable or lovable. And it can be scary to admit you have faults. The need to be perfect and not show any weakness is pretty damn strong. It takes no strength, although it takes incredible energy, to try and pretend you've no weakness or flaws or areas to work on. This objection to Mindset is a defence from a part of you that wants/needs to appear strong and perfect and in control.

I DON'T WANT TO LOSE MY EDGE

Similar to "others need this" is the fear that you'll lose your edge while doing this, or only weak, overly spiritual, non-go-getter hippie wasters do that! (I may have had a little too much fun getting carried away with that last sentence!)

Michael Jordan had a mindfulness coach. I'm Irish, and while *Space Jam* was on my radar growing up, that was about my only exposure to the NBA. Yet essentially everyone around the Western world knows who Jordan is, and I doubt any would say he didn't have an edge or wasn't driven. He was focused AF! His mindfulness coach, the seriously impressive George Mumford, had transformed himself from a functioning heroin addict to the mindset coach of the Chicago Bulls and the LA Lakers. Mumford asked the players to check in and see where their mind was. Was it on their game, or on their opponents, the crowd, their contract, sponsorship deal, or last night's hookup? When are you going to be at your best? When you're bringing your attention to what you're doing or when it's scattered to a million different places other than where you are? Focus is one of the benefits of Mindset training.

Podcast host, philanthropist and self described human guiena pig Tim Ferriss, your edge to a smoking jacket, cycling shorts, or mountain climbing shoes. Rather than being driven by your edge all the time, with awareness you get to decide when and where to use your edge. So, you can still be the focused, relentless individual on the stock trading floor or war room, but you can take it off when it's time to play with your toddler. Without the awareness, your edge is driving you all the time, and a lot of the time it's inappropriate to use it.

_____ IS MY MINDSET/MENTAL HEALTH TIME.

Coming from the gym world, I hear that working out is how people take care of their mental health. While I'm certainly not saying it isn't an integral part of overall health, it's dangerous to rely on something where improved mood and mental well-being is an after effect and not the prime reason. For truly lasting results, you need to work directly on your mind as well as engaging in mood-enhancing activities.

Anything can be used as a tool of mindfulness and to improve your life, or it can be used as an escape. Daily movement is good for you; four hours of obsessive bodybuilding is probably too much. Ditto a drink. I'm partial to a glass of whiskey and love a good cocktail. Going for a drink can act as a shared activity to lubricate social connection. Relying on these things, or drinking to the point of blacking out, vicious hangovers, and a day on the couch wallowing in self-pity isn't healthy.

We humans are also bad at **inductive thinking**—what I mean by this is we're bad at taking the skills from one area of our life and applying them to others. We see people who are way better at us in business but can't apply those skills to their relationships. Or people who are great at relationships, but not so much on the career side. To overcome this, we need to deliberately step back so we can observe our thought patterns. For example, how come I'm so patient when it comes to weight loss but not when it comes to net worth?

External activities are unreliable and likely to disappear over time—2020 taught us that with all the lockdowns. When we sit with our thoughts and feelings, we learn our true needs and are clear on what we get from what we do. Was it bowling you liked? Or seeing your friends, mastering a skill, and having some pure play time? Did you even need those specific friends, or is it the connection and intimacy you need? Knowing your foundational needs, you can then look for other ways to get your need for connection met if the bowling alley isn't open.

WHAT'S MY MOTIVATION?

All the mean, destructive, and hurtful things I've done in my life have been because I didn't know my internal pain, blamed others, or didn't have the wherewithal to communicate in a non-triggering way. That's quite a sentence to write!

When we're in pain, we lash out. We know this, as we can quite easily recall a time when we did this. If everyone was aware of their internal struggle and their external triggers and practiced giving themselves the reassurance and feeling of safety they need, imagine how much nicer we'd be to each other. If we all had our needs met and didn't feel under threat that there's not enough to go around—enough love, money, approval, opportunities, insert-whatever-we-need-here—how much friendlier and happier would we be? We'd act from a place of security and abundance; how better we'd be able to recognise each other's humanity.

When we're in pain, we only see other people as either barriers to our happiness or outright enemies. In our heads they become malicious actors who could solve our suffering but chose not to. When we're taken care of, what's our next instinct? To look out for everyone else. We win and help win.

This is why I believe inner work is so important. Apart from ensuring our planet survives and is able to support life, I think it's the most important project we could work on. Hurt people hurt people. By that same token, free people free people Learning what we need and how to soothe ourselves (instead of wanting and demanding and looking on our fellow humans as competitors for limited resources) can radically change how we show up and what kind of world we create.

WHAT'S MY AIM?

Now that I've convinced you of the reasons to work directly on Mindset, what's in this book and what are the aims? Like I said, everyone says you should look after your mental health, but no one says how. No one has taught you what that looks like in practical, daily(-ish) steps. In short, **I want to solve the problem of "how" for you.**

It's possibly worth revisiting the idea of what Mindset can and can't do for you, to set reasonable expectations. It's unfair if you're not told in advance how much input is required and what the payoff will be. I had a friend who decided he was going to lose one kilogram a week a few years back. (For those who need it: That's a little more than two pounds per week.) This guy was very smart in his IT-based job but had no real education in anything health and fitness related. When I asked him why he picked one kg, he replied simply that it was a nice round number. But losing one kg a week, while achievable, is pretty aggressive and unsustainable weight loss. And without a plan of daily habits to achieve that, he didn't see the progress he liked. After losing some weight, but not as much as his target, he was unhappy with his progress and went back to his old patterns of eating and (not) moving. He ended up a few kilos heavier that year. Had he been prepped in advance for what weight loss he could expect, chances are he wouldn't have been as demotivated and kept going.

If you haven't noticed already, I'm going to relate Mindset work back to fitness, finances, and other tangible things as much as I can in this book to help you understand the concepts. By relating something new to something you already know, you'll learn and internalise the lessons quicker.

Each day, we have thousands of thoughts and feelings, and thousands more small actions. When presented with a change, the two ways we react tend to be that it's too much work or that it won't have enough of a payoff. I hope to get rid of the "too much work" excuse by providing you with the skills that can be applied in less than it takes to read a page or two.

The problem with the "small actions not having enough payoff" argument is that because we don't take *any* action, in the few weeks or months of inaction we lose out on the gains we could have made. And let's be fair, you've probably slid back even further. My old rowing coach used to say that you're either actively moving the boat forward or actively slowing it down—you're never coasting or in neutral.

Bill Bryson, in *A Small History of Nearly Everything*, tells of some algae or some sort that started pumping oxygen into the atmosphere tens of thousands of years ago. Over time, it allowed for all of life as we know it to exist on the planet. Small changes are not only worthwhile but can seriously compound. Albert Einstein is quoted as saying that compound interest is the eighth wonder of the world. Something is better than nothing. And when you build momentum with these small actions, you can always improve and refine as you go along. But waiting until everything is perfect or for the one big fix-everything action is not the way to go.

When, out of the thousands of seconds each day, we slowly start making some of them marginally more healthy and helpful, we overcome the friction of breaking bad habits and creating new (if unfamiliar) thought patterns. And, cliché alert—it snowballs.

In short, the aims are:

- Solve the problem of when to do your Mindset routine.
- Solve the problem of making it part of your life. After all, no one wants to be peaceful for two minutes a day on the cushion and then a stressed mess for the rest of the day.

- Solve the problem of expectations.

WHAT DO YOU GET? WHAT'S THE BENEFIT?

There is so much good stuff in psychology, but like anything, we need a simple approach to it. Now, by necessity, the simple approach will ignore some of the subtleties. In fact, even a complicated, in-depth approach would still miss on some of the intricacies. You may have heard that the map is not the territory. A useful map will help you reach your destination, but it won't tell you all about the smell in the dumpster next to the restaurant, how the right turn looks like you're going into someone's driveway, or that there's an incline on the road. It'll still help you navigate though. The map here, the simple system, covers the bulk of what you need to vastly improve your mindset and mental well-being. But, it won't—and can't—cover everything.

Will it solve all your problems? Yes. Absolutely. One hundred percent guaranteed. *Joking!* Nothing will solve all your problems. Mindset is one component of a healthy, productive life. We'll discuss habits in more depth later on, and which ones add to your overall well-being. But if you take action without being clear on what you want to achieve and why you want to achieve it, you can waste a lot of time and energy. Secondly, if you're changing your habits without working on what's going on inside of you, if you stumble (which you will) you'll need the self-compassion and reassurance to keep going. Hence the importance of building those skills before you work on improving your habits.

The aim is to give you a Self-Care Toolkit—a simple and powerful way to take care of your inner world so you can be your best in your thoughts, feelings, and actions.

What does this mean?

- Peace of mind
- Satisfaction

- Better communication
- Less stress
- Better habits
- Better decision making
- Happier
- Get along with people
- More productive at the right things
- Better relationships
- Able to deal with things
- Calmer
- Reduced anxiety and depression
- **Be that person who's calming and reliable in stressful situations.**
- Be who you aspire to be on the inside
- Be the person your dog thinks you are

I like to boil all the benefits down into three Cs: Clarity, Compassion, and Connection.

The **clearer** you are, the less mentally draining life will be. You'll know what thoughts are helpful and you'll not believe your own bull so easily. Or, indeed, the bull of others. You'll know with more precision what's important, what's helpful, what's healthy, and what actions you can take.

Compassion will benefit you in knowing your feelings, which are really just guidelines on what your needs are. Having compassion for self helps you mind yourself when you're not feeling great and let go of mistakes so you can focus on learning and taking action. Compassion for others helps you get along with them better by understanding the causes of their actions and the universality of suffering.

The better **connected** you are to yourself—your thoughts, feelings, motivations, desires, identity, etc.—the better you can connect to what you do—exercise, nutrition, meaningful work—and the better you can connect to others.

If we are less likely to react to things outside or inside of us, we're freer to choose our responses, and the ones that are best for our health and happiness. It can be done. Like losing weight and building muscle or getting out of debt and building wealth. This is what's meant by **Peace of mind**, which is essentially non-reactivity. And it's not an on/off switch; it's more like a gradient. You'll oscillate back and forth, and with continued practice, your baseline of peace will increase, i.e., you'll be in a better place mentally more of the time and in more situations.

HOW THIS BOOK WORKS

In each chapter:

1. Learn the basic skills and the "why" behind them.

Step-by-step instructions to make the skills very simple to understand and implement. Knowing the "why" behind them also helps buy-in. The more you buy into something the more likely you're going to stay with it long enough to see results.

2. Ingrain them as habits.

Take your time ingraining the habits. It's super tempting to do everything, but ask yourself, what's the rush? When it's super simple to do, add another piece. I recommend about two weeks practicing a mental skill before adding on a new one.

And if you drop one, that's okay. Just readjust and begin again. There's no downside to any of these skills, and you can't really mess them up.

3. Figure out sustainable practice.

It's got to fit into your day. The best times are morning and evening, not when you have to interrupt your busy schedule to switch into meditative mode. That doesn't mean they're the *only* times though! Get curious, play around, and find what works best for you.

4. Integrate them into your life.

We don't want to be great at sitting on the cushion. We want to be great when the pressure is on. Initially, during your formal practice is where you'll notice the immediate benefits, and then I'll offer points on how to bring it into your "real" life.

The ideas in the following chapters are laid out in the best order I've taught to my clients. While it's taught sequentially, ultimately it becomes a virtuous cycle, and like Lisa Simpson's perpetual motion machine, it will eventually just keep getting faster and faster.

Our relationships and how we spend our time dictate the quality of our lives, both the frustration and fulfillment. Since most of our stress *seems* to be from the people in our lives and our environment, it makes intuitive sense to start there. But so much of what works is counterintuitive, so in order to harmonize and maximize our relationships, we need to improve our self-talk to make sure we can coach ourselves through the changes. Also, how we talk to others is a reflection of how we talk to ourselves. To improve habits, we need to first know what our ideal identity, values, and priorities actually are and what we want them to be. That can be scary— both not knowing who we are but also possibly seeing how often we're not acting in line with who we want to be. So, we need the skills of compassion and forgiveness as we embark on that exploration. To have compassion and forgiveness, we need clarity on what's going on in our bodies and in our heads, and so we start with learning how to be aware of our thoughts.

BEFORE WE BEGIN, SOME CAVEATS

Psychology is subjective. There's a lot of competing theories in the field, and who's to say that everything in this book won't be proven false in years to come, refined, or disregarded in favour of something more effective and efficient.

What we think of as pathological becomes normalised and understood over time.

I'm not a psychologist. I like to consider myself like Dan Carlin. He's not an official historian, but his *Hardcore Histories* podcast is the most insightful, informative, and entertaining take on history I've ever come across. My insights come from a fascination with practical self-care strategies and working with people who are motivated to change to find what works quickly and sustainably.

I also have direct experience with this and can teach you from what I've learned and help you avoid the mistakes I've made. Let me be your sherpa on this journey.

A therapist is like a dentist. You need them for the deep cleans and repairs. But you need to put in the work daily with brushing your teeth, flossing, mouthwash, and maybe eating less sugar to begin with. That's where this book comes in—what those daily actions look like.

What I mean is that I'm trying to bridge the gap between formal, academic psychology and practical applications. By making taking care of your mindset as simple and easy as possible to implement, there'll be some oversimplification at times. This might miss some of the subtleties of one thing or another and not apply one hundred percent to one hundred percent of people in one hundred percent of situations.

Maybe you agree that taking care of your mental well-being is important but feel it's not a solo endeavor. I completely agree. Life is always better shared. Lori Gottlieb states repeatedly in her book, *Maybe You Should Talk to Someone*, that your person necessarily need to be a therapist but a friend who can give you wise compassion. So, whether you go with a licensed mental health professional, a life coach, or just someone in your life who'll give it to you straight, having a coach or companion along the way will benefit you to no end.

Am I saying it's all down to Mindset and how you take care of yourself? Anything reductionist like that is oversimplified. And anything too simplified is probably BS. There are genuine "real" problems you're facing, have faced, or will face—loneliness from not having a relationship or being in the wrong relationship; financial trouble from crippling debt or a soul-crushing job; obligations to look after a family member, capital-T Trauma from childhood, etc. We need to improve our real world and the world inside our heads. Either one without the other is just incomplete. In this book, I'm working from the inside out; not ignoring the outside world, just getting ourselves in the best possible state of mind to address the challenges.

THE RESISTANCE & THE JOURNEY

As you begin your journey of introspection, you'll initially be excited. You're (finally) doing something for your mental and emotional health. A few weeks in, the resistance is going to rear its ugly head. I've found that telling people about this ahead of time helps them stick with the habit long enough to see real, lasting changes. Resistance can show up in two forms, internal or external.

There's **internal resistance**. You're rewiring your brain here, and those deeply ingrained patterns are going to push back a little bit. This can show up in the form of skipping days, being impatient with the results, deciding that you don't really need to do this, etc.

When you notice this, remember that this is normal and natural. It's literally part of the process to have some internal resistance to something early on. There'll be self-doubt. Parts of you will convince you that you need to focus elsewhere. It's no different than sticking with savings or diet when you don't see the immediate shift in the bank or on the scales. Being curious and co-opting the resistance, i.e., making it part of your daily practice, will help you through this first resistance.

The second is when the process of looking inward starts to bring to light your fears, your insecurities, your inconsistencies, and all the times you didn't live up to your ideal self. That's going to really suck!

This is going to require a lot of your compassion. This is also how we build up our courage, humanity, and humility.

Courage—because so many people are driven by fears they don't even understand let alone recognise, blindly pursuing goals that may not meet their needs. Always being driven by fear ultimately harms themselves and those around them by failing to live true to themselves.

It can be exceptionally scary to see all the ways we're not perfect, holding ourselves back, living in fear, a mess of thoughts and incongruent beliefs. And it's why people stop meditating. Let me set the expectations for your introspective journey with a little analogy:

Imagine you inherit your dad's old, cluttered shed, and it's the perfect size and shape to be your sanctuary. Be it your home gym, game room, home sauna, whatever! You get all excited to open it up and start clearing it. You can't wait to get rid of all the old junk and dirt and create the dream space exactly how you've always wanted.

Then you open the door and start dragging out the crap! A little while later, you're covered in dirt and grease, you've gotten distracted by odd relics a hundred times, you're starting to lose enthusiasm, and now, not only is the shed still a mess, but there's stuff all over the garden too.

Exploring and taking care of your mind can be like that. We have the initial enthusiasm, and then we start to become aware of our old default thought patterns and emotions. Our initial excitement gives way to a whole lot of discomfort.

It can be very tempting to rationalise why you should shut the door again and go back to other familiar pursuits. But that stuff doesn't go away. It can nag at you and be a drain on your mind, and the space out back still isn't usable. What helps here is compassion, learning how to recognise and soothe your fears. Awareness and compassion go hand in hand, and this is why they're the first two skills taught. It's easier to tune into thought than feelings, so we'll start with thoughts, then follow up with feelings.

It can be tempting to not look at the darker side of our minds for the fear that by unlocking that door we'll be overwhelmed by it. But here's the thing, you're already impacted by it twenty-four seven. The choice is to swim in it or drown in it. You can wade in as far as you're comfortable for as long as you can tolerate—and by doing this, those less-than-pleasant parts of your psyche no longer have total control over you.

External resistance is going to come in the form of some tough, stressful event that's bound to happen. You'll get anxious or angry and then think, "What's the point of all this inner game bull if I still get affected by this?"

If you'd just taken up lifting weights and the bar was loaded to one hundred kilograms (~220 lbs.) above your max strength, it's not that you haven't gotten stronger by lifting—you simply haven't built up enough for that challenge at that point in time. You might be less stressed now when there's a line in Starbucks, but you're not ready yet to stay calm when your boss schedules a one-on-one on Friday afternoon. If, like most of us, you've been in reactive mode for most of your life, it's going to take time to be able to fully deal with all of life's ups and downs. Which leads us to expectations.

YOU CAN'T STOP THE WAVES, BUT YOU CAN LEARN TO SURF. —JON KABAT-ZEN

I got asked once if I felt pressure as the 'Mindset guy' to always be in a good mood. Absolutely not! Because expecting to always be sunny, upbeat, motivated, and positive is setting yourself up for failure. Taking care of your mind will not eliminate the ups and downs of life. You're going to face doubt, feel fear, get angry, and be disappointed. So why do it all then?

A GOOD SELF-CARE PRACTICE WILL HELP REDUCE THE SEVERITY, FREQUENCY, AND DURATION OF THE DIPS.

Severity will reduce because, instead of spiraling when you get knocked off course, you'll take care of yourself better. Instead of reacting to a stressful event by reducing your sleep, eating like crap, not exercising, overworking, not communicating, etc., you'll shepherd yourself through by doing the basics to bring yourself back to baseline. You won't need to wait until you've hit rock-bottom or the problem has gotten overwhelming to make changes.

Taking care of yourself will reduce the frequency as well, because you've built up the foundation and reserves of self-care. You'll also begin to see the early warning signs and double down on what you need to do to stay healthy. And because those reserves are built up, the downs won't last as long as they did.

So, how long do you have to do this self-care malarky anyway? You wouldn't find the love of your life and say "How long do I need to love them?"—you'd look forward to it and to caring for them. And you'd plan on doing this forever. It doesn't need to take up all of your time and energy, and indeed it shouldn't. You're going to move in some way every day until you die; same for eating and sleeping. You're going to maintain and strengthen your relationships as long as you can communicate; and as long as you're able, you'll do something worthwhile. Now you're just adding internal self-care into your daily routine. Let's get started!

Colm O'Reilly

YOUR MINDFUL MINUTE

ALL OF HUMANITY'S PROBLEMS STEM FROM MAN'S IN-ABILITY TO SIT QUIETLY IN A ROOM ALONE.
—BLAISE PASCAL

Taking care of your mind once and for all can seem pretty daunting. With so many facets to it and so much to declutter we can be overwhelmed before we even start. We're not going to tackle everything all at once—that's unfair on you. What we are going to do is start by giving your mind a short restful minute every morning.

From the moment you wake up your brain is bombarded with stimulation from all sides. There's the thoughts in your head, the radio or TV, family members, social media, the noises of breakfast and the neighbours, and that's all before you even leave the house or open up your laptop to start working—which brings YouTube, news sites, email, Slack, etc.

Without taking a purposeful break, your mind is never given an opportunity to sort out the signal from the noise, the important stuff from the distractions, the real issues from the nonsense.

When we take a minute, we're giving our minds the time to settle down. It's also the start of the process of building our self-worth. You're giving yourself a minute because you deserve it. This is the start of a real self-care practice. Out of the 1,440 minutes in a day, just sixty seconds is purely for the care of your mind.

Now, your mind is like a snow globe. And it's been shaken vigorously for years on end! So, when we put it down the first time, we're not going to get super clarity straight away. The whole thing is going to keep swirling. Most people think they've failed meditation because of this, because they can't stop the constant never-ending stream of thoughts when they take the time to pause.

The brain's job is to produce thoughts, much like your heart's job is to pump blood around the body. Try to stop your heart now for a minute. You can't! The same is true with your thoughts. You don't have to try and force your mind to slow down. You absolutely can't. But you can give it the space and time to calm down all on its own.

Over time, the more you put the snow globe down—the more frequently you pause to give your mind some space—the more you'll be able to distinguish the flakes of snow from the blizzard; i.e., the more you'll be able to identify thoughts clearly from the swirl of noise. This is **clarity**.

Imagine you're in the middle of a scrimmage in American football or in a ruck in rugby. You're caught up in immediately what's in front of you, or just trying to keep your limbs safe! That's your brain when it's caught up in a train of thought. The quarterback or out-half can see a bit clearer than the linesmen or the flanker. The coach on the sideline can see clearer still, and the video analyst—removed from the immediacy of it all—can see the clearest. When we take time to notice our thoughts, we naturally become more aware of them and see them clearly for what they are—just thoughts. From there, we can make clearer, calmer, healthier decisions.

You won't get immediate clarity or inner peace any more than one sit-up will give you abs, or one day's investing will make you a millionaire. To give you that expectation is totally unfair. What's likely going to happen is you'll have glimpses of clarity, then chaos. And the second you finish your formal minute, all those thoughts will swarm back in pretty much immediately. The next time you do it, you might gain a couple of seconds of peace from chaotic, unstructured thoughts. Over time, this calm clarity will spread further and further into your day.

Taking just sixty seconds, one mindful minute, your little clarity break, gets over the objection of "I don't have time." No one can't spare one minute of their day. In fact, when I first taught this to my client Paul, he said he literally didn't have a minute. His wife had the kids up before him, and once he dropped his daughter to school, his work yard was only two minutes away. And once he got the yard, the lads were already there so it was straight to work.

Paul suffered terribly from anxiety. He'd never told anyone about the weight of looking after his family. The fear that something might come along to destroy his business (and his status as a provider) caused him no end of stress and sleepless nights.

So, I asked him if he ever checked his phone when he got to the yard. "Always," he replied. Great, here was our opportunity to take a minute. "Just stare at your phone for one minute before you get out of the truck. No one will think anything weird because everyone checks their phone. Because it's only sixty seconds, you're unlikely to get interrupted as well."

He gave it a shot and added an extra sixty seconds when he pulled into his driveway in the evening—again in his truck, this time before he went inside to his family.

After just two weeks Paul's anxiety was noticeably down. Just so we're clear, I'm not making claims that taking a minute twice a day can eliminate anxiety. But this story a pretty powerful example of how small interventions can have a huge impact.

Say you're a full-time mother, and you don't have the luxury of being in the car by yourself ever. Well, enter Jane and the toilet minute. Yes, we took the mindful minute on the toilet! Everybody poops, so everybody has a chance to take a minute on the throne and allow their mind some time to dump the mental crap!

A minute also solves the problem of 'failing' meditation. You cannot fail mediation! If I assign you ten minutes, there is ZERO chance your mind won't wander during that time. You'll get lost in thought. You'll fidget. You'll start to think of all the other more important, more pressing things that need to be done. You'll start to think, "What a waste of time this is," or notice how uncontrolled your thoughts really are. Distraction and discomfort will disrupt the experience for sure.

With a minute, it's far, far less likely this will happen.

Another benefit of the minute is, over time and with practice, you'll develop the ability to rapidly recentre. To get yourself back to your calmest self without needing to remove yourself from stressful situations, get to your meditation spot, light candles, put on some chants, and spend hours inhaling sage and lavender! You'll have trained your brain to recognise thoughts and get itself refocused on the present in a couple of breaths.

WHAT DO I NEED TO DO DURING THIS MINUTE?

The answer is: really, nothing. You cannot mess this up; you cannot do this wrong. That's the beauty of the minute. As long as you're taking time for yourself, you're giving your mind what it needs. From there, you can tweak and refine it to suit what works best for you.

There are only a few prerequisites, and I hesitate to use them, as you'll still reap the benefits even if you don't do these.

The first one is to recognise before you start that you're doing this for yourself and for the good of your mental well-being. That first simple act takes less than a second and is extremely powerful. In that second, you've shifted your mind. You're bringing your focus toward your health, and you're showing yourself some much-needed self-care. If self-love seems too gooey, think of it as self-maintenance.

As for the minute itself, you can decide which option works best for you:

- **Mental Break.** Literally take a time-out from life and give your mind a rest from all the inputs it's dealing with. You can simply set your stopwatch for sixty seconds and watch the time count down. Just a minute where you're focused as much as you can be on one thing, letting your brain run all it needs to do in the background. You don't need to worry if you're doing it right or not. If you get distracted or lost in thought, just return to the clock.

- **Breathwork.** The reason why the breath is used so often in introductory meditation practices is because it's something we have with us at all times. Personally, I like to deliberately slow down and deepen my breathing. It's my little cue that helps me get centred in the moment. When we're relaxed, we take fewer and deeper breaths per minute. The aim is to get us out of panic or survival mode. And this is the very same reason why some people don't like focusing on the breath. The only times they've noticed their breath previously is when they've been in panic mode, and that's where their minds return when they try to control their breathing. So, if this is you, you don't have to use the breath technique. Or you can play around with regular, natural breathing. You can count the breaths, or simply note "inhale . . . exhale."

- **Body Scan.** Simply notice the raw sensations from your head to your toes, or from your toes to your head. You can do a slow scan or run up and down your body quickly. If you notice yourself telling a story about a sensation or judging a sensation ("Oh, I don't like that"; "My stomach is upset because of last night's dinner") try to come back to the sensation itself—tingling, heavy, light, itchy, deep, warm, cold, etc.

- **Sound.** Simply listen and notice how many distinct sounds or subtle noises crop up and fade away from your consciousness. The more you listen, the more sounds you'll notice. Right now, as I type this, I can hear the birds outside, the oven fan going, my dog gnawing at his toy, the distant hum of traffic, the sound of the keyboard. A benefit of listening is that, when we focus on what we're hearing, the internal chatter tends to slow down. Eventually thoughts are going to spring up again. When this happens, you haven't failed—it's what thoughts do!

• **Observing Thoughts.** Notice what thoughts creep up without the obligation to act on them or even believe them. An oft-used analogy is that you're sitting on the side of a river, and each thought is something floating by. You don't have to attach yourself to any of the flotsam. If something you forgot (like sending an important message to a colleague) pops up, then GREAT! You've already experienced an immediate payoff from taking time for yourself. Eventually, you'll notice you have deeper thoughts and moments of stillness. These will vary over time. Some days you'll experience lots of stillness and you'll think you've finally nailed inner peace! The next day, chaos! It's all part of the journey.

• **Open Awareness** is noticing what you're noticing. So, you could start with the breath, then notice a body sensation, then a sound, then a thought, then zone out, go back to the breath, and so on. You've no plan; simply follow what your awareness lands on moment to moment.

The important thing to remember is you cannot fail at this. You're taking time to give your mind some care and exercise, and there are benefits to whatever style suits you. If one stops working for you, switch to another. The key thing is you're taking the time and investing some energy into your mental maintenance.

I need to reiterate this point: You cannot do this wrong. Some tactics will work better than others at a particular time, but they all are net positive. You may need a welcome break from your thoughts that listening or a body scan provides. You may need to invest more into your internal chatter, and this is where watching your thoughts becomes useful. All help. All are healthy. Taking the time is the important thing.

When the minute is up, acknowledge and reward yourself for taking the time to get to know your mind, investing in your mental health, and making your brain a little cleaner and tidier. Mentally giving yourself a pat on the back provides an immediate reward and reinforces the likelihood that you'll repeat the habit tomorrow.

Oftentimes, I'm asked by clients if they can do a guided meditation, listen to music, go for a walk, or stretch out instead. While all of these can contribute to your mental well-being, the aim is not to rely on another external fix. Guided meditations are brilliant, and I avail myself of them. However, you miss out on becoming your own source of mindfulness, introspection, and peace of mind if you don't include some self-directed quiet time. The same is true of any pleasurable activity. Playful rejuvenation time is important, and you can practice being as present as possible during this too. What will help is devoting those 60-120 seconds daily to nothing but the mind rather than having improved mental well-being as a secondary benefit of an activity or something layered onto the original purpose.

WHY ARE WE DOING THIS? WHAT'S HAPPENING?

Every action we take is a vote for the person we are and want to be. When we take a minute, we're telling ourselves that our mental health is important. That we are important. We can put ourselves down the priority order for the entire rest of the day and make everything more important than our health and peace of mind. But for this one minute, we're charging ourselves up.

By taking time daily, we're increasing our self-worth.

Our brains are overloaded with stimulation from the moment we wake up to the moment we go to bed. When we take at least a minute, we give our minds a chance to sort through everything and separate what's useful from what's nonsense. It begins the process of clearing your mental inbox.

So basically, our brains need a break from the overwhelm. Our minds are tired from the constant barrage of stimuli—it's in constant catch-up mode. We've all seen just how cranky and irritable children are when they have stayed up late the night before or missed their nap. Us adults are really no different—we just compensate with a lot of coffee and sugar. We need breaks to be able to perform at our best. It's better if we're either engaged fully or completely resting. But we've all gotten caught up in the semi-focused-lets-keep-going attitude.

Have you ever seen someone you cared about hammer away at the same task without stopping to pop up and look at what they're doing? And you can see that if they just paused for a moment and looked at what they're doing they'd see a better way, or even if the whole thing was worth their time and energy. Well, guess what? You're that same person! But you can take a step back and notice when your thoughts aren't serving you. It just takes practice.

This distance, this space—this is **awareness**. This is what brings clarity. As famed psychotherapist Carl Jung said, "Until you make the unconscious conscious it will direct your life and you will call it fate." We can't even make a decision on whether we need to change a thought pattern or habit until we can see it clearly. We also need compassion, which is the next skill. The minutes you invest in your mind's health develop your ability to notice thoughts for what they are—just thoughts. Then, over time, you will improve your ability to respond to them instead of reacting to them. You'll know which thoughts are worth dismissing and which thoughts are worth investigating.

We're starting with thought because we've access to it. Then we'll go deeper into emotions.

WHAT'S THE BEST ATTITUDE TO HAVE WITH THIS?

TRUST AND TEST

The guy or gal who goes to the gym and believes in their program (even if it's far from optimal) will get more gains than the person who's constantly doubting it. Adopt this attitude. Trusting that you're doing something good for your mind and that your practice is helpful sets you in the right frame of mind. Periodically, you'll feel the urge to review your practice—and that's fine. Just as you wouldn't plant a seed and then dig up the garden to see if it's growing roots, be careful about questioning your practice before it's had time to make an impact. There is no magic pill, no lotto ticket that will bring one hundred percent peace of mind one hundred percent of the time in one go. Day by day, you will increase your peace and happiness baseline by investing in your mind.

PLAYFUL CURIOSITY

Second to this, we want to bring an attitude of "I wonder what this will be like, and what benefits it will bring?" We have enough demands on ourselves to produce and get it right most of the time, so we don't need this when we start taking care of our mind.

When we're curious and playful, we're more interested in finding out what's going on rather than forcing ourselves to be right. I know the perfectionists and the impatient readers will struggle with this, so remember: Out of the 1,440 minutes in your day, you can spend 1,439 of them working on your impatient perfectionism!

CAN I GO LONGER?

Yes, you can take longer than one minute. However, I've tested a lot of different meditative approaches and I always find myself coming back to the minute or two for myself and my clients. It removes the major excuse of not having the time.

There are also contraindications to meditation and introspection.[1] These all seem to occur after elongated periods of silence/attempted mindfulness. I don't want you to use inner work as escapism or get caught up in spiritual materialism. The person who's an addict is escaping life (or more

---

1 "Lost in Thought—The Psychological Risks of Meditation" by David Kortava. https://harpers.org/archive/2021/04/lost-in-thought-psychological-risks-of-meditation/.

accurately the pain of trauma). People who dive into other pursuits that we might societally deem as "good" can also be a victim of this—overachieving and never stopping. The guy or gal who renounces all their worldly possessions and moves across the world to hide in a cave is also attempting an escape. I want you to get the benefit, then get on with your day! Get your needed clarity so you can create (and co-create) your world with compassion. We're not trying to be the best guy or gal at sitting on a cushion!

WHEN SUITS?

Ideally, we want to take our mindful minute as early as we can in the morning, for a few reasons:

- We want to bring our best selves to the minute (even if you're not at your best in the morning it still works for this exercise).

- We don't want it to become another nagging thing on your to-do list, something you need to stop for in the middle of the day.

- We want to do it before the day's tasks have worn us down, the meetings have drained our mental energy, and the to-do list and emails have taken up all our available headspace.

And this brings us nicely to the idea of habit-stacking, which is linking a new habit we want to start with an existing habit. For me, it's stacking my mindful minute with my morning cup of coffee. I picked coffee because I generally have a cup early in the morning, and it's considered a pick-me-up.

By linking our new sixty-second habit to one we already have, it doesn't take up more mental energy. It doesn't become another thing we have to think of. We're trying to reduce mental clutter, remember?

Get specific about what works for you here—is it when the coffee is brewing? When you sit down with it? As soon as it's finished? Then try it for at least a week and see if it works for you. If you don't drink coffee, look at your current morning routine. What do you do almost every morning? When and where will be the best for your new practice?

Which reminds me, take two weeks before layering the next habit onto your current one. Generally, if you try to create too many new habits you'll burn out of willpower. It seems quicker to start doing everything right now, but how is that beneficial when it's only a few days of activity and then a backward slide. Less is more, and the slower path is usually the quicker one in the long term.

Very often, our desire to improve ourselves can come from the belief of not being good enough, and with it comes the urge to get up to standard ASAP. My advice runs counter to this. Instead of thinking how quickly you can reach your goal, or how much you can do, ask what's the least amount of progress you could make today? What's the slowest way to reach your goal? This is key to a sustainable practice, and a sustainable practice will have the biggest long-term payoff.

WHAT'S GOING TO HAPPEN? SETTING EXPECTATIONS

Well, at first, not much really. You won't be miraculously different from before. There'll be no drastic transformation like Steve Rogers when he took the super soldier serum or Diana Prince when she spins into Wonder Woman.

And you may be wondering if a minute will even have enough of an impact.

In Ireland, at the Winter Solstice, it's dark from just after four o'clock p.m. until nearly nine a.m. (16:08 – 08:38). But, minute by minute, the days get a little brighter and longer until summertime, where we get daylight from five a.m. to ten p.m. (04:56 -- 21:57). It happens a minute or two at a time each day.

That's how powerful just a minute is to transform things over time. It's the cumulative impact of small habits. Any habit that seems too easy to do overcomes a lot of resistance to change. If we started out and said you had to focus twenty-four seven on changing yourself, that'd be too overwhelming to even start or too exhausting to keep up. By starting with a minute, we accumulate wins and build momentum.

Think of this study conducted with depressed college students. These guys were at the level where getting out of bed and showering was a chore, their rooms were a mess with clothes everywhere and pizza boxes stacked twenty high. The researchers taped out a one foot by one foot square on the student's desks and charged the students with keeping just that one square foot clean. No further instructions. That's all they had to do.

But the students, with this easy and simple task, started to slowly clean up their desk, their rooms, and themselves. They started venturing back out into the world and attending lectures again. Within a few weeks, their self-reported depression had gone way down. Of course, keeping a taped-off square foot clean isn't a cure-all for depression—or anything else—but it *is* a manageable first step on the journey of self-care..

Our minute is mainly to begin the process of taking time for ourselves. A little pause, done right, helps press the reset button on our constant stream of thoughts. We start at the level of thought because that's the easiest to access as well. It's right there at all times. It's the newest part of the brain, and like all babies, it's crying out for attention at all times!

They say, "Count to ten before you react." It's a trite expression, but . . . the more space we create in our days the less reactive we become, and the calmer, more responsive we are. We build this up each time we add a minute of stillness and quiet time. We're literally building up our buffer, our mental savings account, each and every day. By building in this quiet period in the morning and evening, we're creating space for ourselves to not get carried away by our interpretation of life events.

When you start, you're going to go through what's known as the "Valley of Disappointment." James Clear – author of "Atomic Habits"- talks about this, so all credit to him. It's the time between when you start putting in work on something and when you see rewards. Most of us expect to see a direct correlation between work and results, but in reality, we've got to put in the initial work to build momentum and get past the Plateau of Latent Potential

THE PLATEAU OF LATENT POTENTIAL

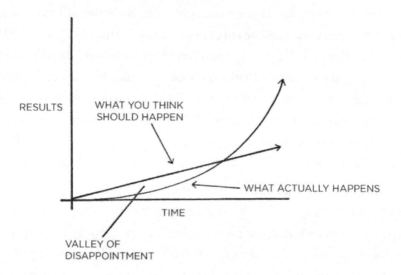

The Chinese bamboo tree doesn't "grow" (visibly) for the first four years. It's just developing its roots. Then, it can grow up to ninety feet in five weeks! I'm not asking you to put in four years of unrewarding work before you see any return on your investment. But there does need to be a degree of trust in the initial stages.

Remember earlier we mentioned at the start of your minute to take a second to acknowledge you're doing something good for your health? And at the end, recognize you've just improved your well-being? These micro-rewards help continue the habit during that first phase when you're not yet seeing major improvements in your life as a result.

That's not to say that you won't feel better for having taken time, you will! However, if you expect to take a couple of minutes for yourself each morning and then nothing in the day will faze you, you're setting yourself up for disappointment. If you're like most of us, you've spent most of your life reacting to things. That habit is going to take some time to turn around. No one loses a hundred pounds overnight. No one goes from indebted to high net worth in the space of the day. Progress can be made every day though!

Finally, one of the ways we can overcome the Valley of Disappointment is to understand that the effort to overcome inertia always seems like it's too much at first. It can very often seem that the reward doesn't match the sacrifice, but consider: There's not much sacrifice in a minute's pause. If you look at your day, you'll see a lot of time wasted waiting for things to happen, switching tabs while one loads, quickly browsing social media while waiting for the elevator, letting your dinner cool while scrolling through Netflix to create background noise. There's a minute in there.

And by taking that minute, you end up saving time later on. You save time by not wasting it on things that don't matter. By seeing more clearly what's a priority and what you can let slide. By pausing briefly before you're overwhelmed and need to take a break, you'll mind will recover its perspecacicty and simply make better decisions. This all comes when we pause before charging into our days in a state of rushed panic.

But, But, But . . .

"I can't quiet my mind."

"I can't shut my thoughts off."

"I can't force peace of mind."

Because it's noisy up in your head when you first invest in Mindset, it's deeply uncomfortable and you might try to get away from it or hope you could just make it stop. You'll never be able to stop your stream of thoughts. Your brain is going to pump out thoughts like your heart keeps beating and your stomach produces digestive enzymes. It's just what it does. In fact, I'd argue that this is one of the big reasons people don't take time for their mind. They feel like a failure if they can't quiet themselves down or stay focused on their breath for ten exhalations. It's worth investing a little time now to explore and debunk some of the resistance you'll have to taking time for yourself.

When you start exercising, you get out of breath. No one who's breathing heavily while running or feels their muscles strain lifting weights thinks they're doing it wrong. It's part of exercise. There's a right level of effort. Too much and you're forcing it, and you might hurt yourself. Too little and you're not going to get any benefit.

What's the right level of effort? Think of training your mind like training a puppy to stay on his blanket. Every time he wanders off, you just gently guide him back to the blanket, pet his soft fur, and maybe give him a treat. Then, when he wanders off again, and because he's a puppy he will wander, you guide him back again. Always with a gentle hand that's firm enough to bring him back. This is the level of effort you want.

Your mind is like a stream, and your thoughts are the flotsam drifting along it. At first, we get distracted and believe every single thought that pops along. Pretty soon, you realize that the surface thoughts are just that, and you learn to let go of them. As you develop, you'll learn to not only see what's going on beneath the surface (long-held unconscious beliefs), but you'll also learn to detach yourself from them as well. All it takes is constant time and friendly curiosity.

At some point, a part of your brain is going to push back, or you're going to "regress" a little. The resistance could show up as a voice telling you that this isn't worth it or necessary, that it's a waste of time. Or that it's not a priority. Or you could forget to take your minute for a day or two. Regardless of how it presents itself, that's completely normal. Recognizing it without succumbing to it is part of the practice. In fact, the last two days, I didn't take my minute in the morning as planned. It happens to us all.

The other big "test" is going to come when something happens and you lose your cool. Then, either you say to yourself or someone else points out that your Mindset training and attempts to calm yourself down have all been for naught. It hasn't been, it's just that the test was above your training for now. The "for now" part is important.

If you've just started in the gym and try to pick up a hundred kilograms, it might be too much too soon. It doesn't mean your twenty-kilogram weights aren't getting you stronger. If you are giving your mind a minute a day for two weeks and then you suddenly lose your job or get in a car crash, that's a big stressor and more than you've planned for, particularly if you already have a lot of underlying stress.

I should also point out that you don't have to "train" your mind. Giving your mind any direct, deliberate attention pays off, regardless of how efficient or purposeful the time is. You cannot get this wrong, only varying levels of payoff. The payoff will change throughout your practice, similar to the payoff you experience in every other area of your life. Sometimes it's subtle; other times it's a big revelation. Sometimes it feels like more effort than it's worth, and other times it feels like everything is flowing perfectly.

"I HONESTLY DON'T HAVE A MINUTE."

If you don't have a minute, can you do thirty seconds? Can you do three deep breaths? Can you do one deep breath?

What we're doing is creating a sliver of silence and a moment of peacefulness in your day. This has been likened to a dark room. We don't need to get rid of all the darkness (busyness, unproductive thoughts, unhelpful habits), we just need to let a little bit of light in. We're dusting off a little part of the window so light can get in daily.

"WHAT IF I THINK OF SOMETHING?"

Do you ever clear your inbox, or to start the day you take care of some quick tasks just to get the clutter down so you can focus on the big, important work? While these mightn't be the main drivers of your career, they're necessary minutiae.

When you start sitting with your mind, these are the first things that will pop up. Your brain is busy and scattered, so anything and everything is taking its focus at any given moment. The more you practice, the more times you'll notice it has settled (even for a couple of microseconds at a time) and the more "important" stuff will arise.

Another analogy that you might find helpful is to think of your brain as a big jar with water and dirt in it. Somewhere in our early years, we learned in school or at home that dirt + water = mud. In the jar analogy, our busy, constant, chaotic thoughts and lives are shaking the jar—oftentimes vigorously. When we first sit to take a minute, the mud just settles down, but it's still mud. There's no clarity. But once we create the habit of sitting with that "mud" for a few minutes regularly, we'll be able to see the water clearing up and the dirt particles settling down.

As that's happening, you notice things bubbling to the surface of your consciousness. Whatever they are, they're the reason you're sitting. They're not a distraction from the breath, or body scan, or quietness you're trying to cultivate. Whatever pops up, regardless of what it is, is a victory. You're now more aware of your thoughts! That's the first step. Over time, we can improve the quantity and quality of these thoughts. For now, we're noticing them.

If "deeper" stuff comes up, like childhood memories, past hurts, beliefs, or narratives that just won't go away, you can take them as important signals to be more conscious about them. You don't have to act on them, or react to them, right away. They're simply useful signposts you can use to direct your attention and your actions for your best benefit.

"SHOULD I DO MORE, TEN OR TWENTY MINUTES?"

I'd genuinely argue no. Not alone anyway. I'm a big fan of guided meditations as a starting point for longer sits, as they keep you focused and give direction. The drawback to them is that your attention is outside of yourself, on the voice of the guide. Your focus is externally driven as the guide is directing your thoughts. What they lack is that essence that can only be obtained by doing nothing with yourself. Just being with your thoughts and nothing else.

If you sit silently on your own for ten to twenty minutes starting off, you'll hit 'failure' by getting fidgety and lost in thought, and it's also most likely too much too soon. I've done sixty minutes for sixty days straight and gotten immense benefit out of it, but that was only after a few years of different forms of Mindset training. There's a reason that "couch-to-5K" is so popular, as you wouldn't start running 5Ks or marathons initially but rather build up to those distances.

I don't think you even need to build up to longer and longer sits—especially if the minute is working for you. No matter what I test, I keep coming back to short, quiet sits as the best recommendation.

BRING IT INTO YOUR DAY

Starting off, I recommend you only commit to the minute first thing in the morning until you get into the habit. But a lot of clients have benefitted from adding in an evening minute. This can either be at the end of the day while brushing your teeth or as you finish up work.

A minute-long mental break when you finish your day can act as a nice mental shift from work mode to home/family/fun mode.

You can expand this idea to take a minute every time you switch environments or tasks. For example, before starting to write this piece, I took a minute; and before my call, I'll take another to allow myself to put aside the previous task and be more present with my Zoom attendees.

A Googler I once knew told me that the company introduced this concept (they called it a G-Minute), and meetings finished 37% faster when they did that. I've tried to find the study but to no avail, but in my own company, giving everyone a minute to settle before starting has definitely led to more engagement.

If you don't have a minute, or for some reason it'd be weird in a particular environment and you'd feel self-conscious, one to three focused breaths can help bring you into the moment.

Periodically, you can also ask yourself, "Where's my head at? Am I focused on the moment at hand, reliving the past, or imagining the future? Or am I judging the present as not enough/not right?" Play a game and see how often you can be where your feet are. This was one of the tactics Mumford successfully used on the Bulls and the Lakers players under Phil Jackson.

It's a gentle reminder to notice what's going on in your head. There's no need to admonish yourself if you're not focused, if you're judging, if you're fantasizing, or anything else. We'll cover **compassion** in the next chapter. And remember, each time you take some time for your mind, you're improving your mental well-being. Each time you *notice* that you're caught up in thought, you've won this game!

WHAT'S THE JOURNEY GOING TO BE LIKE?

At first, you'll get a sense of excitement that you're taking control of your mindset and doing something actionable.

Then, things will start to surface. Remember the snow globe and mud jar analogies? The moment you sit still it's not going to become perfectly clear. As the little bits start to slow down, you can notice them more clearly. Some of these are going to be old memories or patterns of thought you've avoided for years, so it can feel uncomfortable.

Or you could feel a lot of resistance toward continuing the practice. Again, to go back to exercise or nutrition—the sweat, muscle soreness, hunger, and fluctuations on the scales are all part of it. The same is true with our mental fitness.

Along the journey, you are going to stall or backtrack. This doesn't mean you're failing! Not at all. It's part of the process. We all have breakthroughs and slipups in probably close to equal measures. All we need to do is nudge ourselves toward more breakthroughs than backslides.

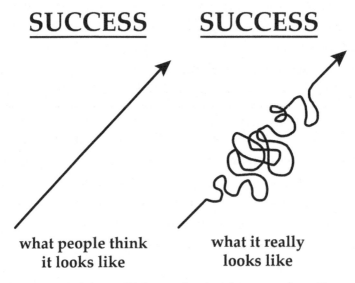

SUCCESS   SUCCESS

what people think   **what it really**
it looks like   **looks like**

The big backslide you'll face is, "Is this doing anything?" Your brain has been dealing with a constant stream of inputs and unfinished thoughts for however many years you've been alive, and you think a couple of weeks of one minute a day is going to sort all that? We're stopping a freight train moving at a thousand miles per hour, and the only way to do that is by slowing that bad boy down bit by bit.

Yes, it *is* doing something. I don't want to say it's dissolving the ego, but we're starting to wake up unconscious patterns that have been running for years, so there's going to be some grumpiness while we shake them from their slumber.

The other aspect is we might reach a point where we get used to it, so we stop "needing it," only to regress in our levels of calm and clarity.

How long do I need to do this? Well, you'll need to eat, sleep, and move every day as long as you live just to stay physically healthy. You'll need to invest in your relationships to be socially healthy, and you'll need to do something meaningful too to give your life purpose. And yes, you need to invest in your mental well-being too.

This is the essence of self-care or self-love. Self-care and self-love can seem tough to do, particularly if you've spent your whole life not taking care of yourself. So, think of the person you care about most in the world. Or, think of your pet. You already know that you are planning to love them forever, so it's not just a one-time thing or a certain season. Now, apply it to yourself.

Or don't think of "forever." Just think of today. Can I give myself this one minute today because I deserve 0.07% of my day to be dedicated to my mental health?

Colm O'Reilly

COMPASSION & SELF EMPATHY

SELF-COMPASSION IS ONE OF THE MOST POWERFUL SOURCES OF STRENGTH, COPING AND RESILIENCE WE HAVE.
—KIRSTEN NEFF

Urgh, Feelings

Am I right? Some people, maybe even us, wish that we could separate ourselves entirely from our feelings or never take them into consideration. Treat them like an annoyance or a distraction. But feelings are an essential signal, and we ignore them at our peril.

If we don't practice tuning in and letting our feelings roll through to completion when we're calm and not in a heightened state, we'll always be at their mercy when they get intense. We'll react, regress, and most likely regret what we said and did while "emotional" because we haven't done the work to feel our feelings and use them productively before we really need to. For some, this can be the toughest mental skill to learn, and this is what makes it the most beneficial.

There's a great myth that you shouldn't make decisions based on feelings. It's completely terrible. All our decisions are based on feelings. Trying to deny them makes us blind to their impact and we'll be dragged along by them. Repressing them can result in those unfelt feelings manifesting in different unwelcome and destructive ways.[2] Pushing down your feelings is like trying to push a beach ball under the water in the pool. No matter how hard or long you try to keep it submerged it's going to pop up somewhere and make a splash!

We sit with our thoughts so we can clear our brains out, sort the important from the unimportant, and get clear on our thinking. We sit with our emotions for the exact same reason: so we can know what our needs are.

Feelings are signals in the body. They're data, not directives. Data we can take on board and then decide what the course of action is. I think when people say not to make decisions based on feelings they're really cautioning against unconscious actions in the heat of the moment rather than making consciously attuned gut decisions. There's a difference between reacting to a trigger and understanding what your body is telling you, then responding appropriately.

Most of us haven't been trained how to fully tune in and process what's going on in our bodies, or, as Jim Dethmer, founder of The Conscious Leadership Grou, says, "fully feeling your feelings through to completion". As a general rule, men are only allowed to feel and express anger (as it's seemingly powerful), and women are told they're too emotional. Because of this, it's going to take time to learn how to tune into the different feelings and sit with them. Luckily, no effort is wasted, and even the attempt to tune into the body's feelings begins to help unclog all those backed up body sensations.

Without tapping into what we're feeling, we decide what to do based on incomplete information at best and inaccurate information at worst. Once we know our feelings, we can understand the needs driving them, and then we can take action that will actually get those core needs met.

---

2 Doctors Bessel van der Kolk's The Body Keeps the Score and Gabor Maté's When the Body Says No go into great depth about how repressing emotions can be linked with serious physical health issues.

Tuning in and fully feeling our feelings are how we deal with negativity and stressful situations in our life. We cannot eliminate negative events, thoughts, emotions, or people! But we can influence the impact of that negativity.

To look at it another way, have you ever shared a problem with someone only for them to rush to the solution without really understanding what you need from them? Or have you done this to someone else? It can seem quite dismissive. We do this to ourselves when we try to rush past uncomfortable feelings to get rid of them rather than noticing them and being curious about what the real need is behind this. This is how we get caught up in reactivity. We feel sad, so we reach for food; we feel lonely, so we go on TikTok; we feel angry, so we take it out on someone, etc. You may have read that the antidote to anxiety is action. This is well-meaning advice, and I'm not saying you just need to feel your feelings and do nothing. Allowing anxiety to fuel your behavior will just result in more anxiety

If we get good at the practice of feeling uncomfortable/intense emotions in a controlled setting, we'll be better equipped when we start moving outside our comfort zone to change our habits, environment (work, family, leisure, etc.), and communication style.

Much like we practice quiet time *before* our minds get overwhelmed, we practice tuning toward emotions before our feelings get overwhelmed. A lot of our (destructive) habits are largely the result of trying to avoid discomfort. If we're not conscious of these, we can slip into unhealthy and unhelpful actions.

From now on, we're going to add a minute to check in with our feelings alongside the minute we spend with our thoughts first thing in the morning. At the start of the day, you're generally not emotionally triggered by anything external so you can get practice in a non-heightened state before you begin to bring this practice into your day. Even if you're generally not your best in the morning, you're at least relatively consistent. This will give you practice tuning into those bodily sensations.[3] You need to tune into your emotions first before you can use them.

So, how exactly do we tune into our emotions?

STEP ONE: NAME THE EMOTION

In order to develop **emotional intelligence**, the ability to use your emotions intelligently, it's first necessary to develop emotional literacy, i.e., knowing what emotion you're actually feeling. The first step is to ask yourself, "What am I feeling right now?" While this seems a super easy question, in reality, you may find yourself unable to identify your emotions. This is normal. For so long we've taught ourselves to tune out our emotional experiences. This could be because when you first experienced them as a child, they were too intense, so your brain shut them down or put other psychological safeguards in place. It could be that your caregivers didn't like how you expressed your emotions, and so they chastised you for this. As a personal example, one of my earliest memories was in fact my mother telling me to stop crying because I'd grow up to be a sullen child. I didn't even know what a sullen child was, nor do I recall what perceived injustice had led to my tears. What I do know is that I interpreted it to mean that my sadness and anger were not to be expressed.

The English language doesn't exactly help, either, when we use phrases such as "I feel like," or "I feel that," which then go on to reveal stories and motivations instead of actual feelings. So, essentially, when we first attempt to name what we're feeling, we find ourselves without the proper vocabulary. It feels like speaking in a foreign language where we don't know the words. (Did you see what I did there?)

This is where a feelings chart or feelings wheel comes into play. When I first started tuning into my emotions, I was so poor at it that I downloaded the chart and made it the lock screen on my phone. So, every time I

---

3 There's not much agreement among researchers on what's a feeling, an emotion, affect, or body sensation. For our purposes, we're going to treat them all the same.

wanted to check my phone, I could check in with my emotions too. I prefer the feelings wheel, as it gives me greater emotional literacy, which adds to my emotional intelligence. Simply go through all the emotions one by one and say, "It's not that, it's not that, it's kinda this, but a little of this too," until you identify the word that resonates with what's going on in your body.

Feelings Wheel

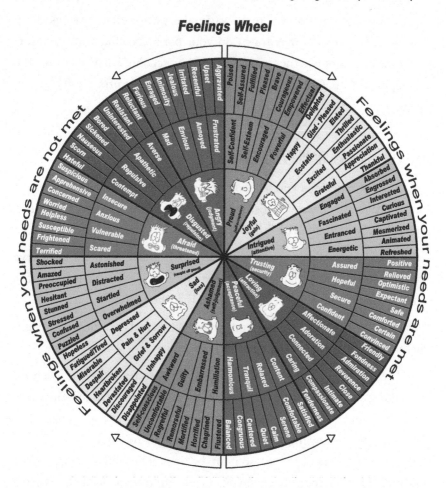

Next up is to use non-identifying language to describe your emotion. The most attached way we can name an emotion is to say "I am sad," as if the entirety of your being is nothing but sadness. That's all there is. "I feel sadness" is a step in the right direction, as it's no longer all of you but a feeling. Better again is "I notice sadness," or "There is sadness present." **This way, we're identifying the emotion without attaching ourselves to it.** It might sound odd at first, but the minor shift in language and the conscious awareness makes it less personal and easier for the emotion to run its course.

Naming an emotion will in no way make it worse! It just brings it into awareness. If you were overdrawn on your bank account, you'd be overdrawn regardless of whether you checked your account balance or not. The same applies here. Once we're aware, we can start the process of clearing the emotion and using it as a signpost toward action.

STEP TWO: REASSURANCE/ACCEPTANCE

A lot of emotions you feel will be uncomfortable. The intensity and the pervasiveness mean you just want to get away from feeling it as much as possible. You might even think, "I don't want to feel this."

Or maybe you're one of those people who have been led to believe that feeling bad, hurt, shameful, or upset are weaknesses of character? So, you try to suppress those feelings or deny that they actually exist?

Emotions, all emotions, are universal. We all feel the whole spectrum, whether we like it or not. (More often, not!)

The first part of reassurance (because we'll come back to it when we start taking action) is letting ourselves know that **it's okay to feel this**. This can be as simple as saying, "This is sadness. It's okay to experience it." It doesn't need to be any more complicated than that. You may need more reassurance (and that's okay too), so it can be helpful to think of, say, a loving grandfather reassuring you when you got a fright from a big dog or when a glass fell from the shelf and shattered on the kitchen floor.

Another way to look at this is accepting the emotion you're feeling in the moment. And it is possible to accept both the emotion and the desire to be rid of the emotion. It's the opposite of judging yourself for having the emotion—which you've probably tried, doesn't really work, and definitely isn't helpful.

Resistance can also manifest in telling yourself this shouldn't have happened, i.e., not accepting the situation. When you tell yourself something like, "This shouldn't have happened!" you're only amplifying your suffering. It's going to take time to practice accepting what's happened and what situation you're in. Understand that, by doing so, you get yourself out of wallowing and into a better mindset quicker. It's a skill. You mightn't be ready to accept that your lover left you for your best friend, emptied your bank account, and stole your dog. You can accept that Krispy Kreme is out of your favorite donut. Start there, then build up to the more intense situations you need to face and accept.

STEP THREE: FEEL IT

Now you've got to fully feel it. This practice liberates you from the unhealthy coping strategies you've had in the past, and from the emotions hijacking your day and your actions. I'm not saying that coping strategies are inherently bad. We all have them. In fact, let's look at two common unhelpful and unhealthy coping strategies.

The first one is **distraction** (or disconnection). Man, do I love this one. I notice discomfort arising while trying to type out this sentence, and I reach for my phone to quickly check social media. Or I open up YouTube to avoid feelings of boredom, sadness, or loneliness.

The other big one is **rumination**; this tends to occur with acute, sharp emotions. You get annoyed, and then you think of all the justifications for your annoyance. You may even fantasize about revenge or relive all the ways this injustice is completely unfair and how you've a right to be pissed off.

By fully feeling your emotions, you don't get stuck in either disconnection or the cognitive-emotive cycle.[4]

So, how do you do it?

Take sixty seconds and notice where the physical sensations of this emotion are in your body. If you're feeling something in the chest, where *exactly* in your chest is it? Is it in all of your chest or just the center? How high and low does it spread? Is it at the front or toward the back? If you're feeling knots in your stomach, notice how the sensation moves around, how the intensity ebbs and flows, where the feeling starts and ends.

Next up, notice the sensation itself. Is there tightness, heaviness, tingling, stabbing, shooting, warmth, cold, fizzing, bubbling, softness? It can be helpful to imagine you're a robot or an alien experiencing the human body for the first time and you're genuinely curious about the sensations that are going on.

When you first do this, you may notice that the intensity is too much for you. After as little as one to five seconds, you may need to escape the emotion. This is normal. After all, you've probably spent decades not consciously feeling your feelings, so you'll be out of practice with this. This is where we introduce a release valve to the overwhelming sensations. There are three that are particularly useful.

- The first is to go back to **focusing on the breath**—noticing the sensation of your inhalations and exhalations and bringing your full attention to them. The breath is largely neutral, so you can focus on that until you're ready to go back to the sensations attached to the emotion.

- The second option is a **soothing touch**. As babies, we responded positively to soothing touches; as adults we give ourselves that same comfort. Now, once I said to a Mindset group I was coaching that the best way to relieve overwhelm was to touch

4 Credit Jim Dethmer - https://conscious.is/blogs/the-cognitive-emotive-loop-what-it-is-why-it-keeps-you-stuck-and-how-to-break-free

yourself —not my best choice of words! Ahem, instead, you can place your hand on the "problem" area and notice the change in sensation. Or you can rub your forefinger and thumb together —another neutral sensation—until you can go back to the emotions again.

• Finally, you can **make fists with your toes.** The great thing about this particular release valve is no one would notice you doing this method of self-soothing. The sensations of your feet don't carry any emotional charge – you don't feel sad or happy or angry in your feet.

You may need to alternate between the emotional sensation and the release valve twenty times or more during your minute. In time, you'll be better able to sit with an emotion. As you do, you'll notice how, when an emotion is allowed to run freely, it dissipates by itself.

Emotional sensations come in waves and rarely last longer than ninety seconds—unless you get caught up in revisiting them or repressing them, in which case they'll metastasize and can last years!

STEP FOUR: INVESTIGATE THE NEED

At the end of your minute of fully feeling your feelings, you're in a place where you can understand what the emotion is telling you. Feelings are signposts or warning signals that a fundamental need is or isn't being met. Fundamental needs include security, variety, growth, significance, contribution, and connection. Jim Dethmer breaks them down into just three—approval, control, and security. Sometimes these words don't quite hit the mark, and we might need to hone in on a subset of these. For example, your need for connection might show up as a need for acceptance, consideration, empathy, trust, or just to be understood. Your need for meaning could be competence, hope, participation, or stimulation, etc.

There is a difference between our needs and our wants. Needs are fundamental; wants are the strategies we use to achieve them. So, my need for significance is fundamental, and I can use writing this book as a strategy to meet those needs, among other things. You might want to go to dinner with your partner, which is a strategy to get your need for connection met. The strategy feeds the need (no pun intended). Connection can also be met through a phone call, a cuddle, or going for a walk together.

If you find yourself saying "I need this to happen," or "I need this person to do this," it's a good signal that you're focused on a want, and not on a fundamental need. The reason we tend to think there's an external fix to our internal state goes right back to the aforementioned baby stage when our needs were met entirely by someone or something outside of us. If you were hungry, you were fed; if you were cold, you were given a blanket. Eventually, you were taught how to walk, talk, and make sense of the world. But before your brain could reason, it learned that, if it had an internal need, something outside of you took care of it. When we're emotionally heightened, we revert back to being a baby and expect a guaranteed fix to come from somewhere else!

In reality, it's most likely a mix of internal and external solutions to your needs. There's the inner part that you're responsible for, and then the real-world actions. For example, you may need to reassure yourself that you're okay and secure, and you'll need to have that critical conversation with your boss. You'll need to work on accepting and loving yourself while improving your body composition. Right now, we're starting with taking care of our internal needs ourselves. We're not ignoring the external part of the equation entirely.

It's going to take time to understand what your needs are, and that's okay. Like learning a gymnastic skill or speaking in a foreign language, it's going to be clunky and awkward at first. In time, it'll refine and become very natural.

Knowing our needs, we can then start to look toward setting and keeping daily intentions.

Needs Wheel

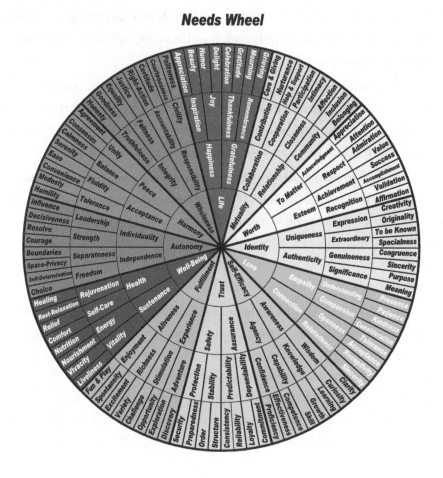

INTENTIONS—SELF-COMPASSION IN ACTION

Daily intentions are compassion in action. It's where you'll use your feelings to direct your activity in order to satisfy your needs and not make your happiness and peace of mind reliant on something outside of you.

Compassion doesn't mean giving yourself the easy option, letting yourself off the hook for all the obligations you've taken on, and allowing yourself to wallow away eating ice cream and watching *Back to the Future* on repeat.

If you love your kids, you ensure they brush their teeth, do their homework, and say please and thank you. These are things that will benefit them; that's **compassion**. Have some for yourself.

The best boss would support you, drive you slightly outside your comfort zone, and make sure you have everything you need. Treat yourself as the CEO of You, Inc., and make decisions accordingly. What's the best action for you to take today, both in the short term and the long term?

Compassionate intentions are your safeguard against the frustration and anguish of your obligations. If you hate your job or your day's schedule looks horrible, your mind will instantly go there first thing in the morning. You may notice anger or sadness; maybe there's some resentment or apathy to your day. This is most likely because your need for freedom isn't being met, or maybe it's preventing connection or excitement in your life.

Intentions are how we build our **sense of agency**—how much control we feel over our day and ultimately the direction of our life. When asked "What would make my day?" or worse, "What would make me happy today?" you'll naturally turn outward and answer, "If they call back," "If the weather is good," "If I get a promotion . . ." and so on. This isn't compassionate, as it's putting your inner state at the whims of fortune. When we ask, "What can I do today that will make my day?" we bring the responsibility and power back to ourselves.

Intentions also balance out against "shoulds." You want to relax, but you think you *should* be doing something more productive with your time. You want to focus on this Zoom but think of how you don't have time to relax! In both cases, we're wishing we were somewhere else, in some other state. With time, you'll be able to be more in the moment than in magical fantasy land. (And you'll notice how often everyone else is somewhere else as well!)

Your intentions and your obligations don't have to be in opposition to each other. You can acknowledge that you have restraints on your time and energy—everyone does! Which brings us back to acceptance.

Acceptance is critical as, without it, we're stuck in a powerless victim state and unable to move forward. Acceptance is understanding and welcoming the current situation as it is! If you find yourself unable to accept the situation you're in, you might be equating it with resignation. Imagine you're driving from New York to Chicago. You get on the road and after a while realize you're driving toward Miami. Acceptance would be to embrace the fact you're driving in the wrong direction, and then look to get off the interstate and turn around. You might have to keep driving farther away from Chicago at first until you reach the exit ramp. Resignation would be to just stay on the course until you reach Miami, even though you really wanted to go to Chicago. And ignorance would be to continue driving south in the belief that you would reach Chicago somehow! You can accept that you can't spend the day watching the entire Lord of The Rings trilogy, and then schedule time to watch it on the weekend. You can accept that you can either go to the gym or meet a friend for a coffee—and make the choice as to which serves your needs better.

When you start with setting intentions, it's vital that you set intentions you're able to achieve. So, start small—stupidly small. So small it seems like it's not going to move the needle at all. **You want to become someone who makes and keeps promises to themself. This is how you build not only your self-agency but your self-worth.**

How often have you created a long to-do list, only to not get it all done? Or even add more items and then have an even longer list get carried over to the next day? Each time you do this you're telling yourself you're the type of person who can't fully accomplish what you set out to do. These subtle and daily failures add up over time to a negative view of yourself.

As with gradual accumulation of negativity, don't forget that incremental change for the better works in much the same way. From the outside, your day may look the same with setting intentions—meetings, emails, admin work, etc. It might only be .00001% different externally. On the inside, you're no longer feeling as trapped but way more in control and deliberate in what you're doing each minute.

Some examples can be:

- Make the bed after getting up.

- Clean the dishes after breakfast.

- Clear five emails (not massively productive but a small win, if needed).

- Leave work at an agreed time.

- Read one page of this book.

As we build our agency, we can take on bigger and bigger tasks and better and better habits. The first thing is to build up the victories.

Start simple and small. The goal here is to set and keep one intention. Then two. Then three. Ultimately, all of them. **Set one to three intentions that you *can* do for the day.** If you set an intention that's too big to be completed in a single sitting or a single day, it's too big. Instead, what can you do? What can you start? For example, you can't write an entire book in a day, but you can dedicate thirty minutes to writing.

Direction is more important than speed. The speed doesn't matter all that much, really. What's the rush? Seriously, ask yourself, "Why rush?" What will you lose/what will you suffer if you don't get this done by this date? It's something I've had to constantly check with myself so much. Set yourself up for success: the skill of setting and keeping intentions is what you need to build first. *Then*, you can start moving the needle on all your worldly goals and aspirations.

MEANINGFUL. KIND. FUN.

I cannot stress this enough: Don't dismiss "easy" or "minimal" wins as a starting point. Much like the Mindful minute mightn't seem like much at the start, it compounds, and it can provide massive benefit. Particularly if you feel discouraged at how little perceived control you have of your day, by carving out even 0.1% of your actions and time under your control, you begin to slowly shift the balance toward greater and greater agency and assurance.

Even with that, clients of mine have often gotten stumped at this point, not knowing what intentions to set. Hell, even I get stumped when I'm unsure what will move the needle of my life or what the greatest act of self-care is for me right now.

The best recommendation is to pick things that are meaningful, kind, and fun.

• **Meaningful:** We all need purpose in our life. The great thing is you get to decide what's meaningful and what you give meaning to. In work, are you laying bricks, building a wall, or creating a cathedral? In your family life, you can decide that playing with your kids or phone-free dinner is meaningful. In your personal life, you can determine that chats with a friend, your workout, or reading are all meaningful pursuits. As you infuse your tasks with meaning, you'll feel greater satisfaction with your life. The more you practice this the more you'll notice daily activities that aren't meaningful and start to drop these from your calendar. But don't sweat about them right now. Ask yourself, "If I could do one thing today that would make it a success, what would it be?" Ultimately, your most important task is whatever ensures your peace of mind, and this will vary from moment to moment.

• **Kind:** There's really no such thing as a selfless act because you feel good when you do good for others. Research has shown that people given $20 to spend on others reported feeling happier than those who spent $20 on themselves. Kindness can be simple acts like eye contact, a smile, or sending your friend a quality dank meme! Start small. One important thing: You can't keep score with this. If you buy your friend a coffee, it needs to be a freely given gift without expecting anything in return. If you're keeping tabs, you'll lose the benefit of the kind act. Don't forget that you can be kind to yourself as well. It's often neglected. Saying no to a task, taking a day off, or finishing that project is an act of kindness. We'll dig further into kindness in a later chapter. For now, it's enough to start with the intention to do one kind thing.

• **Fun:** Play is vital to your health, it's re-energizing. It is not wasteful or sinful. Again, you get to decide what's fun and recharging. You could be going to the gym anyway and decide that's your fun time, or specifically set time aside for your current Netflix obsession. Fun is doing something for its own sake, "without purpose," where you get lost in the activity. If you really need to give it purpose, think of it as charging yourself up so you can do all your super-serious obligations.

"BUT THEY WON'T FULLY GET MY NEEDS MET."

It's quite possible that your actions won't fully satisfy your needs. But how much do you lose, how much have you lost, by not taking any action because they aren't one hundred percent what you want? Getting started and partially fulfilling your needs is what creates momentum. Doing nothing guarantees your needs won't be met, and your agency will decline along with your energy and self-worth.

Another closely related objection is that the initial effort almost always seems not worth it—this can be discouraging even before you start.

In the early stages, gently bring your focus back toward your inputs, not the outcomes. Practice being satisfied with what you did, not what the results are in the early days. We all know someone who is too impatient with results and gives up too early. You can probably think of some novice to your field whose expectations are wildly optimistic, and you try to reign them in.

I'm reminded of a story a surgeon once told me about impatience. She knew that broken bones take six weeks to heal. Yet she expected *her* broken bone to heal in three or four weeks! It was only afterward that she realized the absurdity of her thought process; thinking that somehow her bones would heal quicker just because of magical thinking!

Which leads us to **Assurance**, Part 2!

REASSURANCE (AGAIN!)

When you set a goal, you can feel so much resistance that you're unable to start. Your inner critic is trying to keep you safe, to keep you from failing. And they like nothing more than to get into an argument with you. Because they don't play fair, and know all your failings and weaknesses, they're more than happy to beat you down. In fact, you could go so far as to say they thrive on conflict and derailing your actions. Fighting them isn't the answer. What is? Thanking them for doing their job of protecting you! In its perverted way, it's trying to keep you safe.

Whatever we're afraid of—loss of status, safety, finances, time wasted, not being capable or good enough—is a fear of something that will happen in future, not what's happening right now. It's helpful then to remind ourselves that, right now, in this moment, we're okay. Especially if right now, at this moment, we don't feel particularly okay. Right now, reading this, you're okay and you have enough and you are enough. That's not denying that you might be facing some danger, some risk, or need to take some action in the future in order to continue feeling okay. Right now, you're okay.

And you will be okay. Things might get challenging or even overwhelming in the middle, but ultimately, you'll be okay. Repeating this to yourself is how you build self-assurance. Self-assurance has nothing to do with confidence, as confidence is tied to competence at a task or to an outcome. Regardless of what happens (they say no, your presentation flops, you lose money, you don't win the event) you'll be okay in the end.

Once you've established safety (and it doesn't need to feel one hundred percent safe, as long as it's safe enough to take the first step), ask yourself what you need in order to take action. What do you need?

If it's something you need to hear, tell yourself this! At first, because you're not used to the skill of reassuring yourself, it will feel very awkward and seem like it almost has no impact. You already know what to say because if a child, your partner, or your best friend were in this situation, and you needed to comfort them, you would know what to say. Note that I said "comfort" them. Not "advise" them. The order is important: empathize > comfort (assurance) > advise (action).

If it's something you need, then you can look externally. For example, you might need someone's help or cooperation to get your task done. In the chapter on communication, we'll talk about asking in such a way that people are happy to grant your requests instead of being obligated to fulfil your demands!

IMPLEMENTATION INTENTIONS - A FANCY TERM FOR SCHEDULING

How many times have you said you'll do something when you have the time? Or have not scheduled the important tasks into your planner or Google Calendar, and so they don't get done?

If you've created an intention for the day, you've decided it's important. It's either creating happiness or meaning in your life right now or laying the groundwork for future happiness, meaning, or reduced stress. The next step is deciding when you will take this action.

It's normal to feel resistance to scheduling it in as well. That's okay; you can assure yourself through this resistance too. It might seem like turtles all the way down right now[5], but it won't always be. And even if it is, you'll be okay. The story you're telling yourself is that it's a threat to your freedom. Or maybe that you need more time, more space, more prep work, more help to get started. If that's the case, revisit your intention and reduce it to something you can accomplish. Then you can use an implementation intention to schedule it in.

An **implementation intention** is simply a "When . . . then" or "If . . . then" statement.

"*When* it's three o'clock p.m., *then* I'll make those important calls."

"*If* I don't get loan approval, *then* I'll let the team know."

---

5 "Turtles all the way down" is an expression of the problem of infinite regress. The saying alludes to the mythological idea of a World Turtle that supports a flat Earth on its back.

When the time rolls around, focus only on the action, not the result. Rather than set a target you may or may not hit (e.g., five sales calls), you're actually better off focusing on the *time* you can give to the task (spend thirty minutes on sales calls). Over time, you can refine it to be more and more productive. A lot of time, the process is more important than the result, which is why we focus on action instead of outcomes. Actions are within our control, outcomes are not.

It's worth reminding you that you're not here solely to be productive. There'll always be more you can do or could have done. And you'll have days where you're more or less productive. It's natural and normal—though we often forget this. Your worth isn't tied up solely in your output. All humans have inherent worth, and that includes you!

BABY STEPS

I like baby steps for two reasons. One is, the smaller you can make a task the less intimidating it's going to be, so the less resistance you'll have, and the more likely you'll accomplish it. The second is, have you ever seen how much praise a baby gets for taking a step?

In the grand scheme of things, walking isn't that impressive! I know—it's different when it's your child. But bear with me for the lesson. As a baby is learning to walk, barely balancing themselves, and takes one or two tiny steps, what happens? They receive smiles and cheers and applause! Our baby brains remember that, and it becomes super motivating.

Your baby brain still remembers that, which is why celebrating small wins adds up. Any action carried out is worthy of a little celebration. A mental pat on the back or word of encouragement helps you take the next step, and the next, and the next.

I'm not saying go on a three-day bender or host a pizza party because you replied to one email. But a two-second "good job" under your breath as you finally start to clean the living room motivates you. Celebrate all the wins, as that keeps your momentum going into the next task and encourages you to repeat the same steps again tomorrow. Like all skills, it'll be clunky and awkward at first. The more you do it, the easier it'll become to encourage yourself throughout the tasks.

HOW WE CAN MOAN PROPERLY (USUALLY TO OURSELVES)

Sometimes the frustration, anger, or sadness can boil up, and the urge to have a good moan seems like the only thing to do. This is your need to release pent-up feelings and to be heard and/or understood.

One client, Nathaniel, complained of the times when he kept getting interrupted and wanted everyone to go away with their demands of him. He looked at the clock—four thirty p.m.—and didn't want to work until seven o'clock.

He was irritated (when we finally pinpointed where he was on the feelings wheel). The next step was to work on actually *feeling*. This was tricky because it's not a nice feeling, so we always revert to trying to get away and not feel this as quickly as possible. "Urgh, I feel bad—how can I not feel bad?" (While writing this to avoid the discomfort of accurately expressing the idea, I'll switch over a tab, pick up my phone, take a drink of water, pet my dog, get something to eat, check the word count, and go to the toilet. It would have been way quicker to just feel the damn feeling!)

When I invited him to sit with his feelings he actually answered straight away as to why it's important to fully feel whatever's going on. He said sometimes he gets angry and doesn't want to feel the anger, just justify it. So, he goes over why he's right to be angry. (Anger can feel great because it's got some blame in there, and it feels really good to blame!)

This is called the **cognitive-emotive loop**, and to stop us getting stuck there, we go to the body sensations and let them run their course to completion.

Once we did that, we were free to focus on the core need, which was freedom. The inner story was that by working until seven o'clock, he was losing the freedom to do other things. Now knowing that need, we could decide on some actions that can move him toward fulfilling that need. The first one being that he could simply state that it was his decision to work until seven o'clock, thereby taking back control of his time (freedom) instead of having work demand he stay there (restriction).

Another option was to get his need for freedom partially met; he could work until six o'clock, still an hour extra, and then head to the driving range at six thirty—meeting his obligations and also taking care of his need for freedom. It didn't take much convincing to get him to take the time at the range.

Complaining has its place in allowing us to recognize a bad situation, feel what we're feeling, and move on. If we get stuck in complaining, negativity, or hopelessness, it can become harmful.

No need to say "everything's fine" if it's not. Repressing or denying a "negative" thought or less-than-ideal situation can be harmful. Express what's wrong. The key here is to express it appropriately and in context. Is it a complete disaster, a minor inconvenience, a drag of your mental energy, or something else?

Whenever we express something, we're compelled to define it. Left in our head we can ruminate, and things can get out of control. What might be a minor convenience sours your entire day. Or if it really is a life-altering issue, defining it allows us to come to terms with what the impact will be.

State the facts. State your assumptions. Lay out what you believe the consequences are or will be. As you do this it stops the rumination in your head.

Once you've done that you can identify the feeling, fully feel it so you can get to the underlying need, and then take the action that will start to get your needs met. The need could be to just let out your frustrations or ask for help, or maybe it's changing the narrative about what's happening. Maybe it's removing yourself from this situation or something else entirely.

BUT, BUT, BUT . . .

"BUT I DON'T WANT TO FEEL THIS WAY."

Trying to avoid or suppress negative emotions is a surefire way to make the effects of them worse. Either you'll suffer with them for longer or it comes out in other ways. As Tim Ferriss said as a counter to those saying I don't want to deal with this—you are dealing with this! It's just either going on bravely, authentically, and directly, or it's coming out in other behavior. You can either drown in it or swim in it. Either way, you're in it.

Emotions aren't good or bad, but rather they're signals in response to a fundamental need. The more you learn to accept all emotions the better you'll be. Counterintuitively (there's that word again) you'll suffer the negative emotions less the more you welcome and accept them. But you cannot say "I've accepted this in order for it to go away." It doesn't work like that.

Attempting to numb yourself from these so-called negative emotions means you dull the ability to feel the positive emotions too. You can't turn the dial down on one without the other. What you can do, with practice, is not suffer from the ones you detest and develop the ability to savor the ones you do enjoy.

"I CAN'T THINK OF ANYTHING THAT WILL MEET MY NEEDS OR REALLY MAKE A DIFFERENCE."

This is normal. The resistance you feel right now is your learned helplessness, and over time it will diminish. You're somewhere on the scale of zero to a hundred right now, where zero = completely hopeless and helpless, and one hundred = complete agency over everything. The exercise isn't trying to get you from zero to a hundred in the snap of a finger. It's to build tiny pieces of agency, control, and action day by day. Some days, that needle may only move 0.01%. The other 99.99% is out of your control. You're practicing focusing on what areas are in your control. That's the important thing.

If you still can't think of something, go back and take control of something you have to do anyway. Instead of having to go to work, you choose to go to work. Instead of having to clean your room, tell yourself you want to clean your room. This is what clinical psychologist Jordan Peterson was talking about when he told people to clean their room, and why Admiral William McRaven advises people to start making their bed every morning. (In fact, his book is called "Make Your Bed.") These small acts of agency mitigate the feelings of powerlessness.

You'll still reach a point in your day when you aren't fully in control or don't know what to do, but don't let that stop you from doing what you can do right now.

It's a cliché, but you don't need to see the entire journey, just take the next step. I've often not started something because I couldn't see all the way to the finish line. When you start taking action you can always reiterate as you go on. The iPhone, AirBnB, Instagram, and countless other great success stories went through several iterations to start seeing traction. With you, it's important initially that you take action. Especially when it doesn't seem like it's producing results.[6]

Finally, if you're feeling disheartened or frustrated that you can't take action, lean into this feeling and investigate what the need is. Turtles all the way down.

BRING IT INTO YOUR DAY

Inevitably, you'll hit points in your day where you start to drift again or come to a standstill. Maybe you've nothing urgent, maybe you've "downtime" between meetings but still have a list of things to do. What to do

---

6 Obviously, you don't want to waste all your time and energy with futile action. With the evening practice, you'll learn how to review your actions to see if they're moving the needle forward.

now? Use these four questions to help you determine your next course of action:

- What am I feeling?

- What do I need? What do I need to hear?
  (Remember to reassure yourself!)

- What's the best thing I can do right now?

- What reassurance do I need?

With practice, this only takes a minute. If you're wondering where you'll find this time, it can be done quicker than it takes to look through your TikTok or Twitter feeds.

Colm O'Reilly

FREE YOURSELF WITH FORGIVENESS
IF BEATING YOURSELF UP WORKED,
IT WOULD HAVE WORKED ALREADY.
—UNKNOWN

RESENTMENT IS CORROSIVE, AND I HATE IT.
—TONY STARK

LET IT GO

We're all mentally carrying burdens that weigh us down, take a drag on our mental energy, and force us into repetitive conversations in our heads. Every day, we carry more and more unless we release it. Learning how to forgive yourself and others, to let go of anger, shame, regrets, and resentment, is like taking off the handbrake of your happiness. It's that important. In this chapter, I'm going to show you how.

Every day, you slipup. Sometimes they're minor slipups, sometimes they're major! Maybe you consciously notice it, maybe you don't, but our brains have the uncanny bug of replaying old events—from seemingly small things like conversations during the day and forgetful mishaps to bigger things like major life choices, what-ifs, your regrets, and the times you've been screwed over and hurt. If you've been keeping up your awareness practice (mindful minute), you've probably noticed it already. These regrets, and the stress of replaying them, clog up our mental system.

When working with clients, I recommend they start their evening forgiveness practice as they're brushing their teeth before bed. Some clients have used leaving work or turning off the TV as their trigger to start their evening Mindset routine. Much like brushing your teeth removes the buildup of plaque, practicing forgiveness removes the buildup of regrets and resentment.

The number one reason to forgive is because you deserve to be free of the burden of resentment, guilt, shame, anger, and any other drag on your mental energy. That's it. Forgiveness has *nothing* to do with whether they deserve your forgiveness and is separate from whether they need to face the consequences of their choices. Forgiveness is to stop you from suffering unnecessarily.

Forgiveness, amongst other things, reduces your anxiety, depression, and stress levels, increases your self-acceptance, and frees up your mental energy from rumination/potentially destructive thoughts. We need to psychologically draw things to a close. A lot (if not all) of our issues are because a part of us is stuck in the past stress of a situation. Forgiveness helps put an end to the event, struggle, or even the day itself.

The great news is that it is a stupidly simple practice. You just need to verbalize, "I forgive . . ." or "I'm letting go of . . ." followed by the subject of your forgiveness!

For example: "I forgive myself for not doing the dishes." "I'm letting go of my diet slipups earlier." "I forgive that guy in the shops for trying to physically fight me when I asked him to cover his nose."[7]

Much like when we deliberately take time to sit with our thoughts in a non-reactive way, the very act of making the effort to forgive improves our mental well-being! It's that powerful!

You don't need to be perfect with this. And the good news is, you know how to help someone let go of their day. Think of your best friend. If

---

7 This actually happened! I also forgive myself for the way I said it—maybe I could have been friendlier or maybe I could have ignored it?

they rang you at night and told you they didn't accomplish all they had intended that day, or they failed to live up to their expectations of themselves, how would you respond? You probably wouldn't chastise them. You'd let them know it's okay to be human and help them plan to be better tomorrow. Now we'll take that skill and apply it to ourselves.

Start with small, recent events to forgive and let go—the badly worded email, spilling your coffee, not making your bed, eating that Mars bar. I've found it's best to alternate daily between forgiving yourself and forgiving others.

Oftentimes, you can struggle to let go, or it's not as simple as saying, "I forgive you." The main reasons are:

- You're not ready to totally forgive.

- You imagine another universe where you did everything perfectly. We call this the "Universe of Shoulds."

- Not living up to ideals—next time. Ideals are something to strive for, not a stick to beat yourself with.

- The cost of the failure, still paying the price. What do I need to do to recover from this/make it right?

QUALIFIERS: AN EXCELLENT WAY TO SNEAKILY FORGIVE

Some things are easier to let go while other sins are much harder to forgive. For these, we can add in as many qualifiers as possible.

"I'm open to, one day, only if everything works out okay for me, maybe considering the possibility of starting to think about opening up to the idea of forgiving you."

Add as many qualifiers as you need. Forgiveness isn't forced, so if you feel better only partially forgiving, do that. It's letting go of your burden at a rate that suits you.

If you find yourself unable to forgive, or worse, getting worked up over the incident again, use this time to feel the feelings all the way through. Part of the reason you can't let go or forgive may be down to "stuck" emotions that you either couldn't or didn't allow to run their course at the time.

You can also future-date your forgiveness if you really need to. "I'm upset right now, and in one thousand years I'll forgive this." Whatever helps lighten your load.

Forgiveness can be a messy, partial, and elongated process, and that's totally okay. You can let go of mental weight the same way you let go of physical weight—a couple of ounces at a time.

EMPATHY/FINDING THE MOTIVE

Empathy is the key to unlocking stubborn blocks to forgiveness and is particularly useful when we're continuously ruminating over an event or stuck in judgment. Empathy shifts you to curiosity and understanding. It might bear repeating: Empathy isn't to let them off the hook, it's to help you not be stuck in resentment.

"They're a bastard," or "I'm stupid," aren't motives, they're judgments. Judgments generally close you off to other possibilities. If you struggle to find a motive, ask yourself what would have to make sense about their world in order for them to act like that, or what pain would someone have to be in to lash out like that?

There's a parable that goes something like this: You're in the woods, and you come across a dog. Loving dogs, you go to pet it, only to have it snarl and snap at you. So, now you think this isn't a friendly doggo. Then you notice its leg is caught in a trap, and you shift toward understanding why they're snapping. You still mightn't go near the dog, but you understand why they're lashing out at you, even though it's not your fault they're caught in a trap. Humans also lash out at others when they're in pain.

Saying someone is racist is easy. It could be true. What would someone's life have to be like to dehumanise another? Maybe they grew up poor, with an angry father who was so in pain that he blamed Blacks or immigrants for their station. Maybe they weren't given the education to understand we're all human. Maybe their entire social group was racist and had no opposing viewpoints. With a family, education, and peer group all like that, coupled with the strong human need to be accepted by your tribe, how could they not turn out to be racist? With that understanding it's hard not to be compassionate towards their (limited) viewpoint. That said, please continue to my next point . . .

Understanding a motive doesn't mean you agree with the action. And it certainly doesn't mean you condone the actions. We can understand someone being afraid. Acting out that fear in a violent manner is deplorable, but we can *understand* that someone believed there was no other option other than violence without excusing it.

It's an extreme example to illustrate the point. You can work backward from there to think that the person who was rude to you was simply overwhelmed and panicking. Or you didn't get the work done because you were tired.

We've all failed to live up to our standards and done things that "weren't us." When you investigate their motives with curiosity, you'll see that they acted out of fear or absentmindedness rather than their entire personality being that of a jerk. In a less-extreme example than above, when you drift out of your lane while driving it's because of a momentary distraction or lapse of concentration. When another does it it's because they're a maniac and should be off the road, right?

Once you see that most people most of the time are acting out of fear, you take things less personally. If acting out of fear sounds too psychobabbly (it's a word) think of "avoiding discomfort."

Occasionally, we'll look for an emotional motive where none exists. Hanlon's razor is particularly useful here: Never attribute to malice that which is adequately explained by stupidity. It could be as simple as you didn't have the information at hand. If that's the case, you can very often reach forgiveness by saying "I/They did the best they knew at the time."

EMPATHY RECAP: UNDERSTAND THE MOTIVE
(THE REASONING BEHIND THE ACTION),
THE EMOTIONAL AND NEED DRIVING THE BEHAVIOUR,
AND THE REASONS WHY THEY—OR YOU—TOOK THE ACTION.

ACCEPTING THE OUTCOME

Are you still hoping something had worked out differently? Wondering what life would be like had you said the "right thing," had you said yes or no or a thousand other responses, had they behaved differently . . .? It's normal to replay events. What keeps us stuck is our unwillingness to accept that things did work out the way they did.

If you're unable to forgive or let go of something, notice that unwillingness and then try accepting the result. Remember, acceptance does not mean resignation. And you don't have to accept it fully yet; you'll still benefit from trying. Taking the lesson and focusing on how you can recover/what you can do to move forward will help with this as well.

TAKING THE LESSON

Taking the lesson from something with the aim of improving future action gets rid of the shame associated with "I should/shouldn't have done/said that."

"I should" is just pure shaming. There's no magical other reality where you did everything as perfectly as you should have. Perfection doesn't exist, although it's easy to claim what would have been perfect in hindsight! There's also no perfect version of you in an alternate reality, playing the omniscient judge and deeming your actions as falling short of the mark. The reality is you did the best you could with what resources you had at the time. You couldn't have done better.

Asking yourself, "What is the lesson I can learn from this?" brings more curiosity to the process and gets you closer to dropping the baggage of guilt or shame. (Guilt is "I did something wrong"; shame is "I am wrong."[8])

Our language patterns run deep, which we'll talk about in a later chapter. Right now, we'll practice shifting away from "shoulds" in reviewing our day. And if you find yourself saying, "I shouldn't say should," you can forgive yourself for that as well! I still catch myself editing my sentences. 'Should' is an easy thing to say, and finding an alternative can seem overly verbose. All these subtle shifts add up, though, and are worth the investment. Even substituting "could have" for "should have" will improve your mental well-being.

When you take the lesson, look for something you can commit to trying in future. Think experimental rather than prescriptive. Prescriptive rules can be helpful, and they also can be constraints that stop you from responding to the moment. "I'll try this and see how it goes," rather than "Next time, I absolutely must do this."

You don't need to place the pressure on yourself to be perfect next time; simply commit that you'll try another approach and see if it works out better.

HOW CAN I RECOVER?

Perhaps you're still reliving, ruminating, and beating yourself up because the mistake still costs you? The relationship has been damaged, you're financially hurt, it has caused a physical injury or overbooked your schedule, for example.

---

8 Thanks to Brené Brown for the distinction.

To help you let go of the mistake, ask yourself what action you can take now or tomorrow that will start your road to recovery, Note that we're focusing on what you can do now (agency) and anything that will start it (rather than a total and complete fix, which hardly ever exists).

ENDING SUFFERING

There's a story the Buddha once told, about two arrows: Imagine you got struck by an arrow. The first arrow is the physical wound. You'll feel the pain of the wound and need to address that. The second arrow is asking yourself why the arrow hit you, what you did to deserve it, and wallowing in all the ways you don't deserve this and how it will hurt you in the future.

We revisit and replay events because we're trying to protect ourselves—albeit after the fact. The aim behind this response is to reduce our suffering and heal from it. While it's important to review events, ask yourself, How long are you going to suffer, how long are you willing to suffer from this one event by replaying it, rethinking about it, and refeeling it?

Once you see that replaying it is causing more harm than good, you can commit to slowly letting go of reexperiencing the trauma, bit by bit, at the pace that's right and safe for you.

NOT JUST EVENTS BUT BELIEFS

As you develop your empathy skills, you'll notice that a limiting or unhelpful ~~belief~~ burden can often be the reason why you did something arseways or didn't take your shot. When you identify the no-longer-helpful belief, you can make this the subject of your letting-go practice.

These thoughts can be deeply embedded—**beliefs** are ideas that are accepted as true—so much so that they can be difficult to let go of. Even if on an intellectual level we get that they're not true, parts of us still hold on to them.

Instead of saying "I have a belief that," try the subtle shift of "I hold the burden of," and notice how it changes your attitude to the idea. It's no longer something clinging to you or an integral part of your identity. It's a load you're carrying that weighs you down or holds you back from who and where you want to be.

Again, add as many qualifiers as you like: "I'm committing to slowly releasing this belief, when it no longer serves me, whenever I can notice it and it feels safe to do so, and there's no rush and no urgency!"

A HELPFUL STARTER LIST OF THINGS TO LET GO OF

- Self-Doubt
- Guilt
- Embarrassing memories
- Parents
- Lovers
- Coworkers
- Time wasting
- Words you didn't say
- Chances you didn't take
- A bad day

- Fear
- Past relationships
- Shame
- Siblings
- Bosses
- Employees
- Words you said
- Not being present
- A bad childhood

BUT, BUT, BUT . . .

"I DON'T WANT TO BE LET OFF THE HOOK."

I hear this one a lot. It comes from a deep-seated belief that the only way to take responsibility is through severe self-punishment. If you imagine a scale from taking no responsibility to completely blaming and shaming yourself, this belief comes from the far righthand side of the spectrum.

Look back on what part you are truly responsible for and what accountability you need going forward. Taking on blame for the parts that aren't yours isn't helpful, and we'll return to that when we start working on self-talk.

Accountability is the sweet spot between these two extremes. Accountability is accepting one hundred percent responsibility for the things you're responsible for, no more, no less. Accountability involves accepting that, while we mightn't have acted in line with our highest selves, we did the best we knew at the time. We can take the lessons into the next attempt, do what we can to make amends, and try to improve our behaviour. **Trying to improve, rather than mandating we be better, allows a more compassionate approach instead of letting the fear of perfectionism paralyze us.**

HEALTHY RESPONSIBILITY & FORGIVENESS

LETTING YOURSELF OFF THE HOOK   ACCOUNTABILITY   BLAME & BERATE

"HOW WILL I LEARN THE LESSON AND IMPROVE IF I FORGIVE AND LET GO?"

There's no evidence that suggests that guilt, shame, and other forms of self-punishment lead to a better performance in the future. So, you can let go of that myth. (In fact, you can practice letting go of this destructive belief!)

BRING IT INTO YOUR DAY

If and when you notice yourself stuck in blame, shame, or judgment, ask yourself:

"What do I need to let this go? Is it to fully feel my feelings, to vent, to give myself some reassurance, or take corrective action?"

Doing so will move you from rumination going forward. Of course, you won't be perfect—and you can forgive yourself for not forgiving too!

Colm O'Reilly

HAPPINESS BOOSTERS—GRATITUDE, SAVOURING, & KINDNESS

GRATITUDE

THIS IS FINE. EVERYTHING IS FINE.

Gratitude gets a bad rap. Despite the numerous benefits practicing gratitude can have, it's been oversimplified to sunshine and unicorns and gummy bears and candy floss! Unikitty in *The Lego Movie* is a great example of this: Just think happy, happy thoughts, don't let any negativity creep in, and you'll be super-duper okay, okay?

Toxic positivity is just as bad as being a full-time moany git. Gabor Maté has written and spoken extensively on the physical illness that can coincide with repressed "negative" emotions. That kind of "positivity" is not what we're going for here!

Gratitude brings us back to balance. Let me use a non-fatal car crash as an example. You rear-end someone, or get rear-ended yourself, on the freeway. Pure negativity would be to focus solely on how this will cost you—you'll need to deal with insurers, there'll be a delay while that gets sorted, you might have to forego your holiday to pay the excess and get a new car, at the very least you'll be late to whatever you were driving to. Pure positivity would be "At least you walked away!" in an attempt to ignore the very real issues and feelings that will arise as a result of the crash.

With gratitude, it's not an either/or; it's "and." Yes, now you've got to deal with the repercussions of the accident, *and* you still have your health.

Yes, you have a lot on your plate this week, *and* you love your job. Yes, there are problems with your government, *and* you're lucky to live in a relatively stable society.

This is why we practice gratitude, not to deny our challenges, struggles, and hardships but to accept and welcome the entire picture, not just the negative or the positive.

It's possible to be grateful for what you do have alongside having real problems to solve and strong wants for a better life. James Stockdale was a fighter pilot during the Vietnam War. He was shot down and interned at the "Hanoi Hilton" (which is *so* not part of the Hilton Group). He noticed the same phenomenon as Viktor Frankl did during his stay in concentration camps in World War II: The "optimists" were less likely to survive. Those that believed they'd be liberated by a certain date—say, Christmas—would be disheartened when that date came and went. **Those who survived were those who were able to reconcile the reality of the current situation *and* the belief that, ultimately, they'd be okay in the end.** (You see why developing that sense of agency is so important.)

Gratitude is one way you can appreciate what is going well while confronting what needs to change.

Gratitude also safeguards you against missing out on the good stuff. Our minds tend to dismiss what we already have and have accomplished and default back to looking at what we don't have and haven't achieved yet.

Momentarily imagine yourself homeless and friendless and you'll feel better for the imperfect place and people in your life. Our minds are used to comparing, and all too often you'll compare yourself to someone you aspire to be—the movie star, wealthy neighbour, better athlete, happier couple, etc. You equally have the choice to compare yourself to those without the ability to read (774 million people), people who don't have clean water or indoor toilets (60% of the world population), or anyone who isn't as healthy as you are right now. Practicing gratitude is deliberately and consciously choosing what comparison we're making each day.

It's also work. Your mind's default is to look for threats, and it carries a lot of negativity bias to begin with. If you find yourself exerting mental energy to come up with your list, that's okay. Think of your daily gratitude as burpees for the brain. It's in the act of searching that you reap the rewards. You're literally training your brain to look for the flowers instead of the snakes in the grass!

HOW TO GET THETHE MOST FROM GRATITUDE

To get the most out of your gratitude practice, include it in your morning routine. I'd suggest placing it before you set your intentions, but if you find it's better for you before your mindful minute or compassion time do that. When you practice gratitude, you're more open to possibilities and more likely to see solutions to your issues. Gratitude literally expands your field of vision.

Focus on three key areas to be grateful for: relationships, events, and little things. Add the reason why you're grateful to help tap into the feeling and solidify the benefit.

RELATIONSHIPS

People are your number one source of happiness—and most likely your number one source of stress, but we'll get to that! You can focus on any relationship, past or present. To begin with, start with the happier/more positive relationships to build up your gratitude muscles. Eventually, you'll benefit from including the bad relationships for the lessons they taught you that ultimately led to the good people in your life.

Examples:

- "I'm grateful for my first coach for teaching me my work ethic."
- "I'm grateful for that terrible boss because without them I mightn't have built my dream business."

- "I'm grateful for my dog because he always greets me with a waggly tail."

EVENTS

You get most of your happiness from remembering or looking forward to the events in your life. These can be minor things like a coffee with a friend, a good workout, or bigger events like a holiday or concert.

LITTLE THINGS

Have you ever bought something and really valued it, but over time the joy faded and it became just another possession? Maybe a new coat, your car, or even your favourite coffee mug? Phones are a great example of this—we marvel at how awesome the new upgrade is, and after a little bit of time it becomes just a phone, or we grow to dislike it because it's no longer the latest model. This is called **hedonic adaptation**, your ability to get used to things. By taking some time to reflect on the little things, you can offset this tendency of the brain.

You can use a technique I like to call "negative gratitude" to find something to be happy about. It's easy to imagine if all of a sudden you lost something or it was taken from you. Imagine how you'd feel—either the worry at not having a phone, the frustration of not having breakfast to eat, or the immense grief if your prized bicycle was stolen. Now, imagine if it suddenly returned—how much would you appreciate it?

As a simple example, one morning I walked into the kitchen to see the kettle missing. My morning coffee is something I savour and use to trigger my quiet time. This €10 kettle not being in the kitchen was a little worrisome. My housemate at the time had taken it to top up their bath and had not returned it to the kitchen the previous night. You can imagine how grateful I was when it was returned.

As your practice grows, you can begin to really appreciate everything and everyone you take for granted, and all your good fortune. Once again, we're not denying that you have struggles and hardships. We're merely finding the balance between utter tragedy and complete blissful ignorance. We're essentially becoming more realistic about what's good, and what could be better, in our lives.

WHY...

Naming what you're grateful for is the first step, and then adding in the reasons why you're grateful really cements the emotional benefit of the practice. When you exert the mental effort to explain (even if just to yourself) why you're grateful, you'll be more likely to feel the emotion. Also, putting in the effort helps you with greater clarity on what you get from the relationship, event, or thing. What you're grateful for acts as a signpost for what you value and cherish.

BURPEES FOR YOUR BRAIN

When you start this practice, and even months or years into doing it, you might find yourself struggling to come up with what you're grateful for. You might draw a blank or feel no emotion of gratitude as you make your daily list. This is completely normal. Your brain is wired for threat detection and loves nothing more than to make mountains out of molehills.

Your brain also likes to dismiss things in the past. Part of this is just our need to survive. If you were ever completely satisfied with your achievements, you'd stop striving. By always being slightly dissatisfied, you're always moving toward some goal that keeps you motivated. This makes evolutionary sense but can cause you to miss out on savouring the good moments.

"I'M GRATEFUL FOR X, BUT I WISH IT WAS BETTER."

Early on in your practice, I don't encourage you to add the "but," but we know it will crop up (See what I did there?)

You can use this to direct your attention to how you can make a good thing even better. If you're grateful for your house but wish it were nicer, define "nicer" and determine what action you can do today to move it toward being nicer. Is that cleaning up the living room, moving around some furniture, a big clear out, or looking online to see what's on the market?

"I'VE TRIED GRATITUDE, BUT MY LIFE STILL SUCKS."

If this objection comes up, it's worth asking the question, "How bad is this actually?" and getting specific about what sucks in your life. Is it an annoyance, an irritation, a disaster, a life-changing or life-threatening big deal? This gives you the freedom to admit that some things are sucky. In fact, it's vital that you do. When we tuned into our feelings, we did that. By taking this calmer, more objective approach, we can see it's okay to admit that some things are crappy and give them the correct amount of emotions instead of a disproportionate response. Is one part of your life that's less than perfect taking all the joy out of all the other parts that you're content with?

Finally, you can be grateful for your life *and* want things to improve. The "and" is far superior to the "but." "But" negates anything that came before it, or as therapists like to say, "Everything before the but is BS."

SAVOURING

These elderly subjects were not happier because their life circumstances were better than those of the young subjects; they were instead happier because they had rewired their brains to ignore the negative and savor the positive. By skillfully managing their attention, they improved their world without changing anything concrete about it.

—Cal Newport, *Deep Work*

How often have you looked back on something fondly, only to realize that you didn't really appreciate it at the time? We all tend to forget or minimize what our stressors were in the past, as well as the good times. Forgetting is one part of your psychological immune system—your brain's best efforts to keep you safe and functioning—so I'm not going to suggest that there was some perfect time where everything was perfectly rosy. You don't want to fall into wistful longing for the past, as that keeps you from being present.

We're also wired to never be completely satisfied with what's going on, what we've achieved, or who we are. As mentioned earlier, if we were a hundred percent fulfilled, we'd stop taking action and pretty soon die out as a species. Part of our practice is always going to be aware and accepting that things are never perfect, and that's okay. We'll acknowledge the small bit of discontent while focusing our attention on the positives.

We do that by **savouring—taking the time and investing the mental energy into appreciating what's happening now**. Savouring boosts your happiness, improves memory, and builds your self-worth. You've no doubt ruminated and replayed your screw-ups over and over again. While there's some gain from reviewing mistakes, too much (which is all too easy to do) and you sow the seed in your mind that you're someone who's likely to mess up, or even worse, that you are an irredeemable screw-up!

Without taking the time to savour the wins and the fortuitous moments each day, you're reducing your maximum potential happiness. Because you'll chase the next milestone and the next and the next, expecting that to bring your complete perfect happiness . . . and then ultimately be left with regret that you didn't enjoy what you had when you had it.

As part of your evening practice going forward, reflect back on the day and take a moment (literally a breath or two) to enjoy the wins. Did you make it through a difficult workday and perform to standard? Did anyone bring you a cup of coffee or a sweet treat? Good meal? A great workout in the gym? By recognising the little wins, you build momentum and are better able to go after the bigger wins. And like the morning gratitude, sometimes you'll have to work for this. That's okay; you're literally training the brain to be more optimistic. It has spent its entire life looking for threats (and making them up!) so it's going to need some time to develop this new frame of mind.

Speaking of the bigger wins, it's important to recognise them as milestones and celebrate them. A nice meal or maybe a little present to yourself to mark the occasion is an important way to wrap up the journey. It's very easy to let these things slip by. A friend of mine got the sale of his company over the line after nearly a year of negotiating. He'd initially gone home and just had some cottage pie on an otherwise uneventful Wednesday. I prompted him to purchase something as a present, even just a token gift. Initially reluctant, with a little nudging he did go and treat himself! This didn't negate the sale or financially cripple him, but he now savours his new toy as a reward for all the long nights, big risks, and hard work building and selling his company.

What if you can't find any wins? Amelia and Emily Nagoski in their book *Burnout* explain that after a stress-inducing event, we need to signal to our body that we're safe. Savouring the wins of the day (even if it was "just surviving") helps signal that the stresses of the day are done and allows your body and mind to switch back into rebuilding mode. You've put a knot on the day. While you're brushing your teeth, start with savouring before moving on to forgiveness, and if it benefits you, a minute to let it all sink in.

Some suggested questions to help your savouring practice:

- What was a pleasant surprise today?

- What would I like to do more of?

- What do I remember fondly?

- What am I proud of?

- What moved my life forward today?

"Yeah, but . . ."

In the same way that you practice morning gratitude and can notice a "but" creeping in, this can happen with your evening savouring practice. Initially, it's important that the "but" doesn't disregard or discount entirely the good things that happen simply because they weren't perfect or ideal. Focus on the imperfect pleasure rather than how it wasn't a hundred percent right! Greg McKeown,in his book "Effortless", has said that when you focus on what you have, you get what you lack, but if you focus on what you lack, you lose what you have.

When you get comfortable with this, and you're not rushing past the good stuff to find another area that's lacking or problematic, you can start to use these "buts" (which we've hopefully started to replace with "ands") to direct future actions. What can you do tomorrow that will bring it closer to what you want? Nothing wrong with striving for the ideal as long as you're conscious it's unattainable—and not setting yourself up for disappointment when it's not reached.

As a general rule, savouring and forgiveness can work together to help improve your daily thoughts and actions. Instead of being antagonistic, they're valuable practices that will shift your focus for the upcoming day. All those one-degree shifts add up to a completely different life trajectory.

KINDNESS

Imagine you had your perfect life and all your needs were met. You felt secure and happy and peaceful and safe and confident and everything else inside. What would you do? Most likely, you'd look around and see how you could help those around you get their needs met!

Kindness is reverse-engineering that happiness. If forgiveness was taking the handbrake off your happiness, kindness is the rocket fuel. Recall that when research subjects were given $20 to spend on themselves or $20 to spend on others, the people who spent it on others reported much higher levels of satisfaction and fulfillment. If you're able to take care of others, your brain will naturally assume all its needs are met. Otherwise, why would you be doing it? So, being kind helps you feel secure, peaceful, and fulfilled.

Now, there's a skill to this, and that's what we'll focus on now.

A FREELY GIVEN GIFT

I think credit to self help author and F word fan Mark Manson is due here. Any act of kindness (or "love," as Mark refers to it) has to be a freely given gift without expectation of return. This is how you boost the connection and satisfaction. If you're only buying your mate a coffee so they'll get you back next time, it's not going to boost your well-being. If you're taking a score of how many times you've watched the movie your partner wants to watch, again, it's going to bite you in the ass.

YOU CAN'T SACRIFICE YOUR OWN NEEDS TO MEET SOMEONE ELSE'S

Anything you do can't cost you so much you feel threatened or you lose out so someone else can win. If you do, it'll lead to resentment. Charitable donations will help you feel good if you aren't begrudgingly giving away a portion of your income. If you feel you have enough even with your gift, you'll get the return. If you believe it's causing you budgetary strain, it's not going to work.

Now, there's a difference between a choice you willingly make, like not watching the game in order to listen to someone who needs an ear, and you missing out because they're super needy. From the outside it's the same, but very different, psychological approach. If you choose to spend time with someone because it optimizes everyone's happiness, based on your values, you're not losing out. You get to decide if something you're willing to do.

BE KIND TO YOURSELF

If you're sacrificing your needs to meet someone else's, or because it's easier in the short run, you're not being kind to yourself. Asking how you can be kind to yourself will most likely be very hard at first, as most of us have never been taught how to be kind to ourselves.

Maybe it's taking the pressure off yourself to be perfect. Maybe it's ensuring you take your vitamins, go to bed on time, or put some money aside to pay off your credit card debts. The kinder you are to yourself the more capacity you have to be kinder to those you care about.

BE OPEN TO RECEIVING

Being on the receiving end of kindness can itself be an act of kindness. It feels good to give. If you reject the offer, you deny the other person the chance to do something good. This is especially true when it comes to compliments or verbal praise. How often have you dismissed a kind word by saying something like "Thanks, but I was just lucky." "No, I don't think this dress is that nice." "I still feel flabby." and so on?

When you reject a compliment, you're telling the other person their judgement was wrong. And you're making it less likely they'll praise the next person. Initially, just saying "thank you" to a compliment will feel uncomfortable. When you place your attention on them, instead of you, you'll notice the discomfort subside.

You can express kindness as well by receiving physical gifts or even asking for help.

An important reminder: Kindness is not weakness; it is not subjugating your needs for another. It is not manipulation. It's doing things with a win–win attitude.

METTA PRACTICE: KINDNESS WITHOUT DOING ANYTHING!

You can make your daily kindness practice a *metta* meditation. "Metta," often translated as Loving-kindness, is repeating phrases designed to cultivate compassion, or a friendly attitude, toward everyone.

The default phrase often taught is, "May you be happy, may you be healthy, may you be free from suffering, may you live with ease." But if they're too flowery, you can say, "I hope you have a good day" just as easily!

Sometimes the practice starts with thinking of a friend, family member, or someone you already have great affection for before moving out to people you vaguely know (the barista, the postman, the cashier) and finally to all beings everywhere. Others recommend starting with yourself and working outward.

The aim is to build a default mental pattern of greeting everything and everyone with a welcoming friendliness. Try it as a way of rounding off your morning routine. (We've already started by committing to one kind act in our intentions; this just adds to it.)

OTHER SMALL ACTS OF KINDNESS / BRINGING IT INTO YOUR DAY

Memes. I'm dead serious! Being intentional about making someone smile and sending them something you think they'd like can be your act of kindness. Who doesn't love a curated meme delivery?

Deliberate gifts. Can you buy your friend a coffee? Bring your partner home a small gift from work? Dan Harris, author of *Ten Percent Happier* purposely has his wallet filled with one-dollar notes. No, he's not a frequent customer at strip joints. It's so he has dollars to give to anyone on the streets of New York who asks for one. Whatever they do with the money, or whether they're deserving of it, isn't his concern. The benefit to him of giving helps him recognise that they're people and that we all share a common humanity.

Benefit of the doubt. Recall Hanlon's statement about malice and stupidity. There is a belief that the people in your life know exactly what you want, are able to give you what you want, and if they aren't it's because they're deliberately being mean or cruel. The funny thing about all this is we tend to believe this more the closer we are to someone. More likely, this malicious attempt at depriving you of your needs is the plain fact that they didn't know any better. An act of kindness can be, when someone lets you down or doesn't live up to your expectations, to assume they didn't know any better. Which leads to the next point . . .

Clearly tell people what you want and need. Clear is kind. If you'd like your employees to dress differently (legally, of course!) let them know! If you'd like no phones during dinner, let the family know! The happiest dog is the one who knows where their boundaries are. Humans are just slightly more complicated! By tuning into our feelings, we've helped ourselves get clarity on what exactly our fundamental needs are. The clearer we are in our head, the clearer we'll be able to express those needs to others.

Listening and empathising. Genuinely asking after someone before jumping into the business end of your meeting can be an incredible act of kindness. Or when someone complains to you, confides in you, or even criticizes you (eek!), before you return fire, taking a two-second pause (one breath) and repeating the message back to them shows empathy. Oftentimes, when people hear their own words repeated back to them, they will want to correct what they just said. If nothing else, this allows you time to digest the message and respond, instead of reacting to it. So many people are so caught up in their heads, they don't take the time to listen. When others know that you've really listened to them, you'll be more likely to be listened to in return.

Asking "How can I help/What do you need?" A key habit in my workplace that we've found to benefit everyone is asking at the end of any interaction, "Do you need anything from me?" Now, most of the time the answer is a no. But, it helps build trust and a sense of support that we're all in the same boat.

Telling the truth. Honestly letting people know your thoughts, feelings, and opinions is the kindest thing you can do. There's no need to be brutally honest, as those that claim to be brutally honest are generally more interested in being brutal than honest. Nor is sparing their feelings an act of kindness for you or for them. So, if you really, really hate their home-cooking and can't receive it as a gift, the kindest thing is to let them know you appreciate the thoughtfulness but that it's not to your tastes. Look to phrase your feedback in the kindest way you can.

Congratulations! You've now created a core structure of daily self-care. These practices—mindfulness; compassion; kindness, gratitude, savouring and forgiveness—bookend your day. From here, we'll start working our way outward into our daily life. We'll start with self-talk, which won't be a formal practice but more micro-adjustments to your internal chatter throughout your waking hours.

WE NEED TO TALK
(ABOUT HOW YOU TALK TO YOURSELF)

A lot of the language we use we picked up from other people. You speak English or French or Arabic because you grew up in an environment where everyone around you was speaking English or French or Arabic. But it's more than that. How you express any emotion comes through the words you use and the meanings you have associated with them. Family, fairness, healthy, broken, happy, trauma, etc. all mean different things depending on who is saying them.

Language and meaning gets handed down to us from our families of origin. We learn how to speak to ourselves from hearing how our caregivers speak to us. At the time, we've no real way of filtering out what's useful from what's destructive. Their voice becomes our voice; we unconsciously pick up on how they speak to us and start to speak to ourselves like that, whether it's beneficial or not. As a result, our self-talk is most likely in need of some upgrades!

I'm not saying that the way you talk to yourself completely creates your reality. There is a whole world outside your mind. Self-talk forms part of your filter and lens—whether you categorise events as good or bad, words kind or hostile, people friendly or aggressive, yourself a creator or a victim.

The more conscious we are of our language the more we can decide if it's helpful and, if needs be, change it to be more supportive of our well-being.

Our self-talk is so pervasive, and so much of it is unconscious that updating it takes time. This is why it's okay if we change just one sentence a day. It's also why we started with compassion long before we start adjusting the language we use. When you initially start, you may notice just how often you've been speaking to yourself in a voice that is not kind at all! So, this whole section is another chance to develop compassion and reap the rewards of it.

A good way to approach upgrading your self-talk is to think of it as learning a new language. It takes time to be able to recognise the words, then a little more time to say them, and some more to bumble your way through to simple sentences. With enough time, you'll be fluent. There's no rush in this journey either! Being patient with yourself is further reinforcing your default of compassion and kindness. The following are tactics to help us improve our self-talk, and you don't need to learn and implement them all perfectly in one go.

"THE STORY I'M TELLING MYSELF..."

There's a story of the dad on the bus. It's a rainy Tuesday afternoon, and everyone is just surviving their bus trip home after a tiring day of work when a man gets on with his kids. The kids seem quite riled up, whereas the man seems oblivious to their behaviour. He keeps his head down as he takes a seat toward the front, with his younglings running up and down the aisle shouting and screaming.

Passengers start to stare at each other, giving increasingly agitated glances as if to say, "Who's going to say something?" A few people start to comment out loud how the kids need to sit down and behave, but the dad barely looks up. The general consensus on the bus is that this guy is a bad father.

Eventually, one woman approaches the dad and says, "Excuse me, but do you mind keeping your kids under control so everyone can enjoy the bus ride?" The dad slowly looks up and asks her to repeat herself. "Well, it's just that everyone is annoyed by the kids running up and down the aisle, so can you control them please?"

"Oh, I'm so sorry," the dad quietly replies. "We're just back from the hospital where their mother died, and I guess they don't know how to process it."

At this point, everyone's story about the man has changed. He's no longer a bad father who needs to keep his kids under control. He's a fellow human who needs some support and care.

It's unlikely that in most of our interactions there's going to be such a dramatic turnaround when we let go of one interpretation in favour of another. The key point is that every conclusion we make is a result of a story we tell ourselves.

We make sense of the world through stories—our brain takes certain observations and tries to organise them into something that makes sense. Normally this works just fine. The drawback is the brain is both the narrator and the audience—and tends to believe the stories it creates without question, which can lead to a lot of trouble.

Brené Brown, in her fantastic Netflix special, encourages people to use the phrase "The story I'm telling myself is . . ." I advise everyone to watch it simply because of her great storytelling. But beyond that, the subject matter applies to all of us.

She uses it as an example of how, by using this phrase, we disarm the other person. We're not getting them on the defensive by stating our case as irrefutable truth—which they'll no doubt try to refute. It also keeps us in a state of curiosity and open to other ideas instead of hardening ourselves to our one conclusion. This is the benefit to us, that we're not believing the first conclusion our brain reaches as incontrovertible fact but rather one possible interpretation. Why is this important? If we're stuck in one viewpoint, one meaning, we're closed off for other more positive or helpful ways of looking at it.

I've found that some of my clients don't like using the word "story." When they hear the word "story," they hear "made up." If it's fictional, we're delusional, possibly lying to ourselves, or at least naive and stupid. So, we can use "the narrative," "the conclusion I'm drawing," or "this is what I think it means." Find the version that works best for you.

I'm tempted to tell the story of another tired parent. He told me his daughter was "objectively being annoying." I asked, "objectifying being annoying?" At which point his story became, "I think I was entitled to get annoyed at her behaviour." The whole point wasn't to judge what he initially said as wrong. The words we use to describe things and the stories we create colour our vision of events. This then influences our emotions and how we react. If we're conscious, we have an opportunity to change the story to one that's more beneficial.

So, how do we do this? By breaking our narrative down into the data, judgments, assumptions, and the conclusions.

DATA

What are the observable facts? So much of what we think of data is our opinion, or judgments, of the situation. "They showed up late," is a great example. Did you agree to meet at a specific time? Can you really say the time was wholly and explicitly agreed by both of you? What constitutes "late" anyway? Is it five minutes, ten minutes, twenty minutes? Does it count if they call? Does your idea of late match up with their idea of late?

The fact is, they arrived at 12:07.[9] You thought you'd agreed to meet at 12:00. That's the starting point.

---

9 This might also not be a perfect fact. What if they arrived at 11:55, then got a phone call or needed to use the bathroom? What if you agreed to meet in a large area and it took seven minutes to find each other?

JUDGMENT

Oh man, how we love to judge—just love it. Judging protects us from blame, from being wrong. It even protects us from being vulnerable and taking responsibility for our involvement. It's pretty damn sneaky how often a judgment shows up.

For now, we'll focus on looking at the judgments we assign to others' behaviours. Let's also remember at this stage you're probably beginning to notice how often you don't clearly know your own goals and motives. So, trying to pinpoint someone else's is most likely going to be way off. What motive have you assigned to this action? For example, did he do this because he's a jerk, because he clearly doesn't care, because he's mean and vindictive, because he's forgetful, because he's an idiot, because he devalues you?

If you want to get fancy with it, look at fundamental attribution error and recall the driving scenario from earlier. When we're driving and we drift into the other lane and nearly hit someone, it's because we were momentarily distracted (circumstances made us do it). When someone else does it, they're a maniac and shouldn't be allowed to drive (personality made them do it).

A worthwhile digression here is to talk about how we ultimately want to free ourselves from judgment. When we're in judgment, we've already made our mind up about something, so we're by definition closed off from alternate viewpoints and possibilities. Judgment narrows our vision and disconnects us from other people—even ourselves. The more disconnected we are—from the present moment, the world, our thoughts—the more we'll suffer and not know why.

We judge because it absolves us of responsibility. It can feel really good to blame and shame someone else. Now, here's the rub. We tend to judge in the areas where we're prone to shame about ourselves. Judging someone's appearance, dress, actions, etc. are all areas where we're trying to armour up against feeling that vulnerability.

So, we can co-opt our judgments to reveal areas we'd benefit from exploring. We judge where we're prone to shame in ourselves. For example, we hate lateness because to us lateness means irresponsibility, and we don't want to be irresponsible. We judge another's looks because we're self-conscious about our own beauty standard. We judge someone's parenting because we're worried about how good of a job we're doing.

When you notice yourself saying "They are," use this as an opportunity to reframe the judgment into simple facts. Try and see how curious you can be instead of applying a judgment.

ASSUMPTIONS

We all make assumptions; we're all working off incomplete data and working largely in a "wicked" environment. David Epstein describes wicked environments in his book *Range*. A kind environment (as he describes it) is one where the rules and consequences are always the same. Chess is a perfect example—same board, same number of starting pieces, same way the pieces move, and everyone has one go before their opponent moves. A wicked environment is where the same action will not always produce the same result. In American football, the same play is going to feature different players, different reaction speeds, different levels of fatigue, different individual outcomes etc. Life is a wicked game by Epstein's definition. That's not to say that life itself is wicked!

Bringing your assumptions into conscious awareness helps you understand that you don't have all the evidence or know the complete picture. It also opens the door to check in and see what you think the other person's assumptions might be. (Once again, bringing us back to an open, curious frame of mind.)

Did you assume they could make it on time? That there were no delays in transport? That they found parking without a long wait? That they didn't get held up leaving on time by their family or boss? That there wasn't an accident or a traffic stop on the road?

CONCLUSIONS

What does all this mean? What are the **consequences** of this? What are you projecting into the future? What actions is it "forcing" you to take? What is this going to cost you? In our lateness example, does it mean you'll miss your flight home, or that you're not important to them, or you need to end the relationship and all the hassle that will cause?

Consciously working your way through the conclusions can also help when your mind has simple created a BIG BAD! I was working with a client recently who had no conclusion to their fear story other than something bad would happen. By defining the likely outcomes, we can investigate the probability of them happening and also decide what needs to be done to keep us safe.

Once more, by deliberately breaking down the story you're telling yourself, you can see more clearly your blind spots and give yourself opportunities to improve your understanding.

The whole point of this is not to prove you wrong. It's not about right or wrong and certainly not about who's right and who's wrong. It's not about finding all the ways you're a dumbass or don't know what you're talking about. The whole point is a skillset to allow you to develop greater clarity and compassion. Clarity in that you're seeing where you're assigning motives and making assumptions, helping you see your blind spots. And compassion is the attitude we bring. We've all thought "I didn't know" or "no one told me " to absolve us of any mistakes we've made. Now we can assign this in a broader, more understanding and forgiving way to ourselves and others.

DEEPER DESTRUCTIVE STORIES WE TELL OURSELVES

Going beyond your mate being late to coffee or your coworker talking over you in a meeting, what other stories do we tell ourselves? The story that your problem is unique and unsolvable isn't helping you. What else?

- "I need to fix this *then*."
- "I need to fix this part of me (to be happy, loveable, complete, acceptable, worthy) . . ."
- "I'm just the way I am."
- "My problem is unique."
- "This really is going to be the worst thing ever."
- "It's unsolvable."
- "No one understands or will understand."
- "This is the only way."
- "My stress is really caused by something outside of me."

For some of these, the THINK filter is another approach to gently and compassionately deconstructing harmful self-talk.

THINK

"The story I'm telling myself" is useful when our internal voice is analysing and judging other people. When we have a thought about our-selves, we can use the THINK filter as a tool to start breaking down your beliefs and thought patterns to investigate if they're constructive to your peace of mind.

IS IT TRUE?

Your brain defaults to believing that the stories it has created are true. It's incredibly exhausting to doubt everything you see and hear, so we default to trusting that story. Most of the time it works fine, and this is what allows us to get caught up in Marvel movies and enjoy them.

When you find yourself upset as a result of a story, the first question to ask is "Is It True?" Byron Katie's "The Work" has helped thousands of people drop unhelpful stories that have kept them in suffering by asking this question. Her four questions are:

1. Is it True?

2. *Can you be absolutely certain it's true?* I love this one because introducing even the tiniest bit of doubt opens us up to more curiosity and openness.

3. *How do you react—what happens—when you believe that thought?* Showing us how we're feeding our suffering by replaying the same thought again and again.

4. *Who would you be without the thought?* Once more, exploring the idea that our thoughts, not the situation, are more responsible for our suffering that we initially assume.

For learning purposes, just start with asking *"Is It True?"* and notice what the response is. Notice, don't judge. You're not here to catch yourself or berate yourself for believing a lie or anything like that.

Does this mean everything you think is BS? No, that's a pretty strong reaction, and just because something isn't one hundred percent capital-T Truth doesn't mean it doesn't have a value. A map isn't a one hundred percent accurate representation of the territory, yet it still has value. Our thoughts may start as ten percent true and gradually get closer to the Truth over time.

IS IT HELPFUL?

If the thought is true, and most of the time it will fail this test, is it helpful? Yes, your sister-in-law is a bad driver. As evidenced by her crashing your car. Is focusing on this helpful right now? It's true you're under a lot of pressure, but is saying "I can't cope" helpful? Does it keep you in anger or pity or move you toward reassured action?

Most of the time, your self-talk won't make it past these two tests and you won't need to continue. Of the thousands of thoughts and self-reflections you'll have during the day, you may get upset at how few of them are speaking to you in a kind voice. This is why we spent the time building our compassion, kindness, and forgiveness before we started working on our self-talk. If you only retroactively improve one or two thoughts in a day, that's progress. Bit by bit they'll add up, and eventually the balance will tip toward a more supportive and encouraging inner dialogue. Stick with it!

IS IT INSPIRING?

Does this motivate you to take compassionate action or keep you stuck in the mud?

IS IT NECESSARY?

Do you really need to focus on all the ways you or someone else has messed up right now?

IS IT KIND?

Meanness is you being defensive. Kindness is strength; remember that. Kindness is not manipulative neediness or letting someone play you for a sucker. Maybe you have an obligation to let someone down: a breakup, dropping someone from the sports team, firing an employee. It's almost always possible to be honest and kind. Look for a way to express the thought in the kindest way possible.

THINK is a high standard for thoughts to get through. It's high because you deserve to treat yourself with the same care you'd treat your puppy. By deconstructing thoughts, we stop them endlessly looping in our mind. What's left is the calm, quiet, peace of mind you want, which provides the fertile ground for better thoughts to germinate.

NO ONE MADE YOU ANGRY

Being able to curiously look at our self-talk and reasoning requires us to not be caught up in the moment. Where this is hard is when we're angry and caught in a loop of justifying and feeling that anger. Marshall B. Rosenberg, founder of Nonviolent Communication, describes anger as the tragic expression of an unmet need. When there's anger, it's an emotion of lack coupled with a judgment.

It starts with conflating the trigger of your anger with the cause of your anger. Somebody may *trigger* it, but no one is the *cause* of your anger. No one "makes" you angry. Drop the phrase "makes me angry." In fact, work on dropping the phrase "made me" altogether and see how often you're surrendering your agency to something outside of you.

You can argue that a lot of the concepts we talk about in this book are just natural human shorthand. Phrases such as "It feels like" when not describing feelings and "makes/made me angry" might seem harmless enough. To use an extreme example, one cigarette won't cause lung cancer. Enough, over time, most likely will.

These thousands of micro-decisions add up. To stem the tide, you need only address one or two of them a day and they'll begin to accumulate. Remember: marginal gains—one skipped workout, one month overdrawn, one unkind word—probably won't make a difference. Over time, though, all these small votes compound into a much different outcome.

The judgment of the other person making you angry implies wrongness on their part. Your brain will no doubt invest energy in reasoning why they're wrong, why you're right to be angry, all the ways they've hurt you, and all the ways you don't deserve this transgression and that they deserve to be punished.

When angry, look at the *need* underneath it. If you'd like the other person to behave in a certain way to help you get that need met, ask yourself what reasons you'd like them to have for behaving that way—do you want them to do it with resentment, or compassion?

For more, read *The Surprising Purpose of Anger* or watch the video on YouTube.

YOU SHOULD REALLY STOP USING THIS WORD

If there's one word you really should stop using, it's "should." "Should" is shaming; "You should have known better" is drilled into us at an early age. Maybe, but we really didn't know any better, did we? "Should" implies this parallel universe where you knew perfectly what to do, even if it was your first time, and always executed perfectly. And that perfect universe can see into your imperfect universe and is judging you pretty harshly for your failures.

When you say you should or shouldn't have done this or that, you're focused on the past, on how you were wrong, and possibly punishing yourself.

You might be thinking you don't want to let yourself off the hook by not saying "I should have known better" or "I shouldn't have said that." From the THINK filter above, how can you change the language to something more helpful than "should"?

"Knowing what I know now, next time I'll do things differently." Yes, it's more verbose than "I shouldn't have done that," with the optional "that was pretty stupid of me" thrown in. You can shorten this down to, "In future I'll . . ." Even replacing "should" with "could" changes the tone.

Taking yourself out of the past—where you ruminate on all the ways you should have been better—allows you to be more in the present and focused on the immediate future, which is where you have agency to show up and be different. You can't change the past; or as Ant-Man said, "*Back to the Future* was a bunch of bullshit."

A NOTE ON JUDGMENT & SHAME

Shame gets embedded pretty early in life, particularly around all the things we should or shouldn't know or say or do (although nobody told us in advance; we were just expecting to know these rules and follow them perfectly).

Shame isn't guilt. Remember: Guilt is "I did something bad." Shame is "I am bad." It's guilt so deeply internalised that it becomes part of your identity.

Shame is a defense mechanism. In a weird, way it frees you from expressing certain desires. The malware program of shame can't distinguish between healthy, normal desires and destructive desires. It was laid down before you could tell the difference between the two.

Shame requires secrecy, silence, and judgment.

Think of some of your biggest fears—the ones that you haven't told anyone. When you say them out loud, when you bring them to light, they sound ridiculous. All our fears do. By keeping them hidden, we allow shame to grow on them like mold.

When we're in judgment, either about ourselves or others, if we look underneath, we'll see some form of fear or shame.

You can see this in outspoken anti-homosexual advocates who are found out to have secret lovers of the same sex. This is an extreme illustration of how we judge where we ourselves are prone to shame. Sometimes we judge because we're afraid of that thing and want to be the opposite, and sometimes we judge because we are that thing and are afraid of being seen.

Knowing this, you can use your judgments as a learning tool. Whenever you judge something or someone, look to the reason behind that judgment. Look for the fear, and in there you'll find your growth opportunity.

HAVE TO? WANT TO?

Up there with "should" is "have to," simply because it disempowers you. When you have to do something, you're trapped and your need for freedom, or autonomy, or significance, isn't met.

"Have to" is a great get-out-of-jail-free card because someone else is forcing you to do something, or deny yourself, or be somewhere. It allows you to enjoy being the victim. Like so many of our styles of thinking and talking, it's a convenient shorthand. By replacing "have to" with "want to," you'll begin to uncover the reasons why you're taking on obligations. Now you can see that you want to work because it provides security, or meaning to your day. You want to work out because it's healthy. You want to spend time with your parents because you want to be included in the will!

By eliminating the "have to," you gain greater clarity on the payoff of your actions. All behaviours have a payoff, otherwise we wouldn't do them. Maybe you're doing things just to avoid hassle, and this gives you an opportunity to see how, by avoiding one uncomfortable argument, you're causing endless internal resentment.

If you can't jump from "have" to "want," try simply saying "I am." For example, instead of "I have to work on Monday," you say, "I am working on Monday," as a statement of fact rather than restriction.

I USED TO . . .

You don't want to lie to yourself. And you also don't want to reinforce behaviours you're trying to change. How do you reconcile the two? By using "I used to . . ." and "I'm working on . . ." or "I'm getting better at . . ."

Let's say you want to be more punctual. It lines up with your values, priorities, and ideal identity. Putting your tardiness in the past tense is one small step toward the timely person you want to become. "I used to be late, and I'm working on my timekeeping," acknowledges that you had an issue with time management and are actively working on improving it. Saying "I'm just never going to be late again," is setting yourself up for failure. And in your heart of hearts, you know that's not true.

BELIEF TO BURDEN

This exercise is less to do with our day-to-day self-talk and more to do with our deep-seated, limiting beliefs. If you spend some time thinking about it, it was most likely not a conscious decision to adopt that belief in the first place. Either it was handed down to you directly, you interpreted something a caregiver had told you, or you had a negative early experience and drew a conclusion from it.

To help you let go of that belief, try replacing the word "belief" with "burden." A belief is something deeply held, and it's accepted as fact. A burden is something you're carrying, and it's implied it is weighing you down, or holding you back, and is possibly unnecessary.

The simple shift loosens the grip over the self-limiting beliefs, allowing you the mental room to reduce the drag on your potential.

IF I TRULY LOVED MYSELF, WHAT WOULD I SAY & DO?

Seth Godin wrote an insightful blog post called "The World's Worst Boss,"[10] and I'll quote a bit here: "If you had a manager that talked to you

10   https://seths.blog/2010/12/the-worlds-worst-boss/

the way you talked to you, you'd quit. If you had a boss that wasted as much of your time as you do, they'd fire her. If an organization developed its employees as poorly as you are developing yourself, it would soon go under."

Jordan Peterson, in his book "12 Rules for Life", wrote an entire chapter on treating yourself like you're someone you are responsible for caring for. He cites how often people will ensure their dog gets their prescribed medication more than they'll do it for themselves. Even people after waiting years for kidney transplants and enduring painful lengthy dialysis will not take all of their immunosuppressants. In fact, my good friend always, always makes sure his wife takes her multivitamins but frequently forgets to take his own. It's crazy when you think of it!

Peterson argues that the reason we do this is our **inner critic**—the part of us that keeps a detailed log of all the times we've failed to live up to our ideal selves—berates us and tells us we're unworthy of self-care and good fortune.

Kamal Ravikant, in his book "Love Yourself Like Your Life Depends On It", puts it the strongest way, in my opinion, by phrasing the question, "If I loved myself, truly and deeply, what would I do?" The "if" removes the possibility that maybe you don't love yourself right now. It temporarily silences the negative, critical parts of you so you can start making decisions that are best for you.

Maybe you really don't love yourself right now. A therapist I worked with talked about self-love like this: If she asked you to go down to the bus stop and love some random person, would you? No! Because you don't know them well enough. That's the same with you. But you can start to get to know them and find the parts you love. Find and nurture those parts you love.

Love is so powerful in Ravikant's question because of its intensity. We can all imagine loving someone or something truly and deeply. Love is caring. Love is an active intention, and it's deliberately putting your energies into increasing the happiness and decreasing the suffering of whoever is the target of your love. And it can be you. **You can act as if you love yourself until you really do love yourself.** Treat yourself like someone you love.

I will admit, though, that this question misses the mark for some people. And I'm trying my best to avoid slipping into flowers and unicorns. So, I offer you a more palatable alternative.

"If I were acting in my best interest, what would I do?"

You can use this question when faced with indecision, or when you find yourself with an open calendar and multiple options to spend your time. Couple this question with "Am I trending in the right direction?" and "What small action can I take now to move me toward who I want to be?" each day and notice the positive momentum add up.

Acting as if you love/care/support/are friendly toward yourself is a key component of reaching the point of truly loving yourself. Couples counselors often employ this technique. Before ending a relationship, they'll ask participants to devote themselves to being the best partner they can be for the next three months. This often rekindles the relationship. We can apply this same principle to ourselves. It can be work at times, particularly when you feel unlovable or when the effort seems like it greatly outweighs the reward. The reward comes through the compounding effect of repeated daily loving actions.

BRING IT INTO YOUR DAY

You're now at the stage when your morning and evening practices are bleeding into your daily life, and the self-talk skills in this chapter will provide structure to it.

Please remember that changing patterns *takes time*. There's no rush; you'll improve quicker and more permanently the longer timeline you give yourself. Initially you're only going to retroactively notice that your self-talk wasn't healthy or serving you. Over time, that gap will diminish, and you'll be able to gently correct yourself.

Recall this example: When you're training a puppy, you continuously and repeatedly guide it back to the mat it's meant to stay on. You don't berate it for straying; you just gently move it back. Again and again. This is the best way to improve your self-talk. Besides, if beating yourself up worked, it would have worked by now.

Start around mealtimes; review and note how you're talking to yourself. What stories are you believing? Does your self-talk pass the THINK filter? If you were acting in your best interests, if you were in charge of making sure you were as happy, productive, successful, and peaceful as you could be, what would you say to yourself and what actions would you take now? It could be as simple as choosing the water for your health (or even the Coca-Cola because you want to savour the taste).

Next up, work on self-talk during your commute. Then, try it when you begin to notice the areas and times you're prone to stress. Bit by bit, your self-talk will improve and eventually a more supportive dialogue will become your default.

A final note from the brilliant Zen Buddhist teacher and author Cheri Huber, and something to remember:

IF THE VOICE IN YOUR HEAD ISN'T SPEAKING TO YOU WITH COMPASSION AND KINDNESS, IT'S NOT *YOUR* VOICE.

FIXING YOUR TRUE NORTH— IDENTITY, VALUES & PRIORITIES

No one wants to get better at just meditating. You want to improve your life off the cushion. Our aim isn't to be our best for a minute either side of the day and then a stressed mess the rest of the time! We want to bring the clarity, compassion, kindness, and forgiveness we've learnt into our daily actions. It's why we started building ourselves up from the inside first—and doing so in stillness so we can bring these skills into our lives.

Once that foundation has been laid, now it's time to understand who you ideally want to be; get clear on your values and priorities before you start seriously changing your habits and environment.

Intuitively, it makes sense to start with habits. Habits without a clear understanding of the meaning driving them either won't be sustainable or won't bring you closer to the peace of mind you are seeking.

Yeah, yeah, find your values, be who you want to be. I know you got stuff to do and obligations out the wazoo . . . If you don't have a measurement for who and how you want to be, how can you tell if you're getting closer to that goal or moving farther away?

How many times have you seen people in your life who pursued a goal with religious fervour only to be left feeling empty inside? Or idiots who drive for the next level and the next level and are never satisfied with what they've reached? Success without a clearly defined definition of success is not success. Most of the time people—including you and me—are pursuing goals because that's what everyone else in our circle is doing, or we're trying to escape some discomfort.

With awareness, you'll be in a much better place to pursue goals that have personal meaning and significance. Think of it like this. Let's say you're in Florida, and you hate Florida. So, you move to Alabama. But you don't like it there, either, so you move to Arkansas. Again, not where you want to be. Do you want to be in New York, Seattle, or Cleveland? Determining your ideal identity, what really matters to you, and what your order or priorities are, is deciding what your True North is. From there, you can begin to take steps in the direction of where you want to go, rather than just "not here." The process of determining these is the inflection point from inner to outer work. How we bring ourselves from the cushion into the real world.

You need to have built up some time gaining clarity on your thoughts, tuning into your feelings, and having the ability to be compassionate and forgiving, because if you don't, you can get quite disheartened and frustrated when you draw a blank trying to determine who you want to be. Which you absolutely will do the first time you do this.

It can be scary and unnerving to realise you don't know yourself so well. As Dr. Kristin Neff, the world's foremost authority on self-compassion, said, you're a mess, but at least you're a compassionate mess! Now, let's keep the compassionate part and start tidying up the messy part.

Ultimately, when you've dialed in your ideal self, you can use this as a litmus test for your habits. You can ask yourself, "Am I moving toward where I want to be?" and adjust your behaviours and surroundings accordingly.

IDENTITY

If you've ever watched the hilarious classic *Tropic Thunder*, you'll see a scene where Ben Stiller questions Robert Downey Jr. on who he is: "I'm the dude playing the dude disguised as another dude! You the dude who don't know what dude he is!" Robert Downey Jr., playing Kurk Lazarus, playing Sgt. Lincoln Osiris, is afraid he might be nobody!

It seems bizarre when you think about it, but you've probably invested very little in defining who exactly you are. Sure, you could take a Buzzfeed quiz to find out what type of cocktail you are, or what character in *Friends* you are. Or maybe you can take a personality test. Granted, the latter is more informative than the former, but have you ever defined who you are yourself?

Why is this important? **Knowing your identity is critical to your self-acceptance and self-validation. In early life, you're told who you are and who you should be. So, taking time to identify just who you are is valuable. Not someone else's definition—yours.**

Your identity isn't fixed, and it has room for growth and development. But it can't be completely nebulous either. You are a person; you have certain dreams, hopes, aspirations, and fears.

Two obvious examples of identities are vegans and those who identify themselves as religious. Vegans don't debate daily if they should eat meat or can drink cow's milk. They just don't. It's not a sacrifice or restraint for them; it's their choice.

Someone who identifies as Christian will have a certain number of rules they live by. Whether they call themselves a Roman Catholic, Presbyterian, Follower of Christ, etc. will go a long way toward how they view themselves in the world and what they do/don't do. And, of course, someone who identifies as a Cross-Fitter will have an aversion to wearing shirts!

Identity gives us positive constraints. For example, people who identified as "voters" were more likely to vote than those who identified as "people likely to vote." We like being congruent with what we say, so when we define ourselves, we're more likely to act in line with that definition. You don't work out because you have to, you work out because that's what a healthy person does. You don't budget because you have to, you budget because that's what a responsible person does.

Who you are isn't fixed. We inch closer to who we want to be with small, almost imperceptible shifts, much like how you grew up or how your hair length changes over time.

You can start this practice by looking at the roles you play in your life. Say for example you're a father. From there, add an adjective to who you are—are you a loving father, an attentive father, a caring father, a strict father, a distant and cold father? (Probably not the last one.) The definition is your standard and not someone else's judgement imposed on you. Only you can answer if you're living up to your standard, and this can only be done when you define what that standard is.

You're not "just" a father in the example above. What commonalities exist between the roles you play as a dad, worker, friend, teammate, son, etc.? You are not your role—you are who you show up as in your role.

WHAT "RULES" DO YOU LIVE BY?

Knowing what your rules are, which you may have never taken the time to define, can help you dial in your identity. What do you strive for? Do you always like to read, watch sports, drink a litre of water a day, save ten percent of your income, do the laundry on given days, pay someone to valet your car? Each rule tells you a little bit about yourself.

You don't need to discover and define every single one of your rules right now at this second. Simply observe your actions—which is bringing awareness to your day—and note what they are. Do you not drink coffee after noon? Do you read the news or avoid it entirely? Do you stay off Twitter? Call your mom weekly? The more you notice, the more you'll be able to see if these actions are in line with who you are—and if they are, what they mean to you, about you.

WHO DO I NOT WANT TO BE?

I cannot stress this enough: This practice can really stump you. It can scare the bloody hell out of you, and you can find yourself absolutely stumped and dumbfounded when faced with the question, "Who am I?" (It's just occurred to me that Zoolander asks himself this question, too— so maybe Ben Stiller's entire career was an attempt to self-identify? But I digress.) Anyone who's ever had to fill out a dating profile or introduce themselves to a room full of strangers knows this terrifying moment.

When you're faced with this blank canvas, it is super easy to become overwhelmed, disheartened, or even angry with yourself. This is why we introduced compassion practice before identity practice—so you can lovingly guide yourself through it.

And just like with daily intentions starting small and doable, you can make it easier on yourself by asking "Who do I not want to be?" I recently texted a client with these options: Start wild, like I'm presuming you don't want to be an axe murderer? A heroin user? Someone who beats their dog?

The act of defining yourself, rather than what you define as, is what gives you self-worth, assurance, security, and peace of mind. Who you are is a fluid concept, and it's perfectly okay to update who you are.

WHO DO I WANT TO BE?

What's your ideal self? How do you want to show up in the world? What attitude do you want to have more of? Do you want to be happier, more athletic, wealthier, calmer, be more of a reader, voter, leader, carer, a better friend?

Before we move to habits, it's important to know who we are and who we want to be. Now, the important thing is practice compassion and forgiveness if you're not there yet. Ideals are something to guide us, not a standard to prove how we're lacking, inadequate, or unworthy.

The important question after we define who we are and who we want to be is, "Am I trending in the right direction?" and "What *small* action can I take now to move me toward who I want to be?" These are now the questions to guide your morning and evening reflections. It's the trend that counts, not the scorecard at any one point in time.

VALUES

If **identity** is who you are, your **values** are what you say yes and no to, what excites you, and what repulses you. There's large overlap among the concept of identity, values, and priorities. That's in part to allow you freedom to define yourself without being overly limited to too few words. We're all richer than just one facet of our personalities or job titles or societal roles.

A major cause of stress is when we act out of line with our values. If honesty is important to us, we won't feel comfortable with lying, even little "harmless" ones. And the more you practice honesty, the better you'll feel about yourself.

Look at the list here and start by picking two to five values that resonate with you. Say them out loud and notice if there's a shift in your body sensations when you say them. No list is going to be complete, so you're of course welcome to pick a word that isn't here.

LIST OF VALUES

Accountability	Achievement	Adaptability
Adventure	Altruism	Ambition
Authenticity	Balance	Beauty
Being the best	Belonging	Career
Caring	Collaboration	Commitment
Community	Compassion	Competence
Confidence	Connection	Contentment

Contribution	Cooperation	Courage
Creativity	Curiosity	Dignity
Diversity	Environment	Efficiency
Equality	Ethics	Excellence
Fairness	Faith	Family
Financial stability	Forgiveness	Freedom
Friendship	Fun	Future generations
Generosity	Giving back	Grace
Gratitude	Growth	Harmony
Health	Home	Honesty
Hope	Humility	Humor
Inclusion	Independence	Initiative
Integrity	Intuition	Job security
Joy	Justice	Kindness
Knowledge	Leadership	Learning
Legacy	Leisure	Love
Loyalty	Making a difference	Nature
Openness	Optimism	Order
Parenting	Patience	Patriotism
Peace	Perseverance	Personal fulfillment
Power	Pride	Recognition
Reliability	Resourcefulness	Respect
Responsibility	Risk-taking	Safety
Security	Self-discipline	Self-expression
Self-respect	Serenity	Service
Simplicity	Spirituality	Sportsmanship
Stewardship	Success	Teamwork
Thrift	Time	Tradition
Travel	Trust	Truth
Understanding	Uniqueness	Usefulness
Vision	Vulnerability	Wealth
Well-being	Wholeheartedness	Wisdom

Next up, define what they mean to you. Oftentimes, the same word can mean different things to different people. For example, when we did this with our staff one day, two people came up with the value of "fairness." For one, it meant everyone was treated the same regardless of the value they brought to the business. For another, it meant that everyone's rewards were in line with their contribution to the company.

The act of defining your values cements your ownership of them. As you do this exercise, you might notice the first values you pick aren't quite right—that you want to include them all or none of them are really jumping out to you. That's okay as well. It's the practice that matters—you can't get this wrong! As you continue the journey of defining your values, they'll become clearer. And much like your identity, they're not set in stone for life. You're free to change your mind as you go deeper with your practice and life more consciously.

PRIORITIES

Setting our priorities is "the one decision that eliminates a thousand decisions," in the words of Tim Ferriss. It's determining ahead of time what's important and what takes precedence. If not, outside forces will dictate our time and our schedules, which means that the "important" things in our life will end up getting table scraps or nothing at all.

There's the famous story of the philosophy professor and the glass jar. He first fills the jar with rocks and asks his class if it's full. Then he adds in some pebbles, then finally sand. If you fill the jar with sand first—representing the unimportant minutiae of life—then you'd have no space for the rocks—the important stuff.

To determine your priorities, start by looking at your calendar; where is your time going? Now, more time does not automatically mean a higher priority. It's merely data, not a death sentence of how incongruent you are with your priorities.

Some aspects of our day require more time. We need seven to nine hours of sleep, for example. Meals and commuting may take up another couple of hours. Quality time with your loved one might be "only" one hour in the evening, whereas work is eight hours, but that doesn't automatically mean work is eight times more important than loved ones.

When you know what your time is spent on, you now have a list of all your activities. Regardless of the time commitments of each, you can list out what they are as a priority.

From there, you can work outward to more abstract concepts. Is making an impact a priority for you? Is it health, happiness, family, career progression, sporting achievement?

Discovering this is a huge win if something you want to be a priority hasn't been given time and energy. Now you have the ability to start carving out some time for it!

Nir Eyal, in his book *Indistractable*, talks about how you should focus less on achievement and more on spending time doing what you intended to do during that time. Recall my writing example: Instead of getting three pages written during my writing session, I'm better off investing the thirty minutes writing and not switching tabs when I get stuck.

All too often, he argues, the important stuff gets pushed down into the "dead" time after all our calendar obligations are taken care of. So, the important people and activities in our lives get whatever energy we have left over after we do all the stuff we have to do. Your fitness, family, or hobbies get the crumbs of you.

To counteract this, if you have a new habit that's important, or a priority you want to devote more time to, or a relationship that needs more nurturing than you're currently giving it, it's time to look at your calendar to see where you can make the time instead of waiting for the time.

What's important is you put time aside for the creation of the new habit. "When I'm free" or "When I'm less busy" is a fantastic lie we all tell ourselves. Life never gets less busy or frees you from your obligations unless you make the shift in how you plan and spend your time.

Knowing your priorities now means that if there's a conflict you have premade the decision. Say, for example, there's an optional work event the same night as your son's recital. If you value family over career, the choice is already made. This is over simplistic, as, remember, you're in charge of what meaning you give things. If your kid is a teenager and really doesn't want their uncool parents there, and the optional work event will give you a chance at a higher paying job that you can use to upgrade your house for your family, you can make a different decision.

The key is, you're making the decisions in line with your priorities. You have guiding principles that will allow you to understand the reasons for your choices. You no longer "have to"—you're deciding. Agency, baby, agency! It's a fantastic feeling when you are doing everything you want to do in a given day, versus everything you have to do. It could be the exact same list of priorities, but when you know you're in control of the meaning you give them, the attitude you bring and payoffs/tradeoffs of everything, it's mentally liberating!

To give an example, my priorities are:

1. My peace of mind

2. My dog

3. My mission

The list then expands to my circle, my family, my people, ultimately caring for everyone. It took me a long time to realise that if something disturbs my peace of mind, everything else and everyone else would suffer as a result. And that's the rub with this: *you* have to be your number one priority or everything else will get less than it deserves.

In first aid exams, they ask the question about who's the most important person in the scene of an accident. Most answer that it's the person who's unconscious, or not responding, or bleeding. But the answer is—it's the first responder.

You're the first responder to everything you value in your life and all your priorities. This course is built as a fake-out—to make you the number one priority. When you're at your best, everyone gets your best.

Now, if caring for someone fills you full of energy, if bringing someone coffee or helping them gets unstuck from a problem fires you up, do it! We're not saying ignore the needs of everyone else. By the same token, martyrs have a limited life expectancy. If you notice you're losing enthusiasm for what normally does get you excited, recharge yourself first!

As we know by now, recharging yourself is the most impactful thing you can do for *everyone* in your life. Define your priorities, making sure you're not forgetting *you* among everything else! Once you know your priorities, the next step is to determine what actions (habits) from you are needed each day to ensure they're topped up.

HOW OFTEN?

This is not a one and done, it's an iterative process. Determine values, act in line with them. Reexamine and reset. Repeat. Repeat. Repeat.

On your first attempt at defining who you are, what you stand for and what's important to you, you'll most likely be completely stumped. You won't have a clue how to define yourself, which values you rank higher than others, and what your priorities are. You'll see your calendar and energy expenditure is completely out of whack with what you say matters. Spoiler alert! Almost everyone's is! That's okay! This is really going to be a big exercise in compassion for you! And others!

The important thing is you begin to shift your focus toward how *you*, not how the world or anyone else, determines what's important. Have you seen a trend here? You can't get sitting with your thoughts wrong, even if you still get dragged around by them. You can't get attempts at self-compassion wrong, or your gratitude list, or acts and intentions of kindness. The value is in the focused, deliberate attempts.

Initially, I'm suggesting you take a daily attempt at defining and refining your identity, values, and priorities as part of your morning ritual. Over time, a monthly and quarterly focused review will work. Of course, you're welcome to refine what works for you.

Take a minute right now to lean into the discomfort of the unknown and begin the process of you being the one who defines you, compassionately reminding yourself that direction is more important than speed.

BRING IT INTO YOUR DAY

You're not trying to "catch" yourself not living up to your identity, values, and priorities; you're periodically giving yourself a chance to course correct. I don't know if it's true or not, but apparently if you froze a plane's direction at any one time, it would be off course like ninety-nine percent of the time. It's constantly course correcting. And it still gets there. You can do the same thing by asking yourself these questions with compassion:

- Is this who I want to be?
- How would I behave/what would I do if I were at my best?
- Is this in line with my values?
- Is my day lining up with my priorities?

IDENTITY, HABITS & ATTITUDE

Most people start at the habit level to change their life. The idea behind it lines up nicely with Christopher Nolan's Batman: "It's not who you are underneath but what you do that defines you."

It makes intuitive sense, and most people operate purely from the external world: "If I change this, then this internal shift will happen." Again, we need to operate in the world, and I'm not suggesting that everything exists in your head. I'm still arguing for going out and fulfilling your mission (how you define it) and seeing where you fit and how you can improve our world. Heck, writing this is my attempt to not only clarify what's in my head but to also change the world.

What can happen is you can fall into the trap of performing habits without understanding the underlying motive or reason. This can either lead to a lack of fulfilment or results you weren't hoping for. Matt Fitzgerald, in his book *How Bad Do You Want It?* talks about the attitudes runners brought to training. Those who said, "This sucks, I'm out of breath, it's a terrible training run" had a different physiological stimulus to those who said something along the lines of, "This is great, I'm out of breath, this training run is getting me fitter." Same run, same heart rate and training stimulus, but a different attitude, which led to a different response.

Knowing what we're aiming for, we can see if our actions and attitude are moving us toward that goal. James Clear, the undisputed king of habits, states, "Every action you take is a **vote** for the type of person you wish to become." It's important you first define who you want to be, then align your habits with that person. A frugal person doesn't debate whether they should save, they just do. So, if your ideal identity is responsible, and you define part of that identity as frugal, you'll save, starting today, with just one dollar.

Now that you know who you want to be and what's truly valuable and important to you, let's take a look at our daily routine and environment.

Colm O'Reilly

HABITS

SUCCESS IS THE PRODUCT OF DAILY HABITS— NOT ONCE-IN-A-LIFETIME TRANSFORMATIONS.
— JAMES CLEAR

Finally, we can start improving all those frustrating and stressful areas of our lives!

Without a strong sense of who you are and who you want to be, the clarity of mind to understand your actions and the intent behind them, coupled with the compassionate self-talk to guide yourself out of the comfort zone (and forgive yourself when you slipup), changing your habits may just be busy work without any internal payoff.

Or, as so many of us have done, it can lead us to chasing goals we never set for ourselves. Humans are memetic creatures (I love that word, "memetic," not least of which is because it contains the word "meme")— we copy each other. It's how we learn. The dark side of this is that we can chase goals that don't mean that much to us because that's what the people around us are doing. Am I trying to get the promotion because that's what someone else wants? Am I buying the latest computer/bike/car because all my friends are?

This is why we held off looking at our daily habits, outside of our morning and evening routines, until now. Backed with clarity, compassion, and courage, you can start to create the life you want. The difference is you're in control, and it's built through love and abundance rather than fear and scarcity.

SMALL, SUSTAINABLE CHANGES

Throughout this entire book I've asked you to make changes: one minute, one thought, or even one word at a time. The reason is sustainability. Anyone can do a burst of inspired activity. What you want is something that doesn't require massive willpower, that isn't at the mercy of your mood, your calendar, or your expanded circle.

We'll look more into willpower and reconciling our inner selves in a little bit, but for now, you want to be able to say of any new habit, that you have 10/10 confidence that you can execute it as often as possible. If you have only 8/10 on the confidence scale, make it smaller. So, maybe you don't know if you'll be able to get to bed by ten p.m. each night. Push it back to eleven p.m. and then slowly creep it back by five minutes at a pace that allows you to not miss any days or believe you're missing out on life by going to bed early.

With any habit, we tend to want an almost immediate payoff. So, we look at the effort versus the reward. If we don't see a reward or think it's not worth the effort, we don't start. This virtually guarantees we won't get what we want. When you start, ignore the payoff and focus purely on the activity, trusting that you'll be able to adjust your strategy as you continue on.

My dad and I at my mam's suggestion of putting €100/month away for a deposit. We worked out that it would take about thirty years to get the down payment, provided of course house prices stay where they are! But she had a valuable point. Start putting something away! Even if it's only €1/month, the habit begins to compound. Yes, €1/month won't get you a down payment. It will start the savings habit. And is infinitely better than going into the red each month. Every quarter I readjust my savings amounts so that I know I can live and save and the amount continues to grow. (It's well over €1 now.)

SNAPBACK EFFECT OF WILLPOWER

One major reason why you want to start with stupidly small habit changes is because of the snapback effect when willpower burns out. If you've ever sworn off sugary snacks and gone cold turkey only to reach breaking point after a stressful day and eat ALL. THE. SWEETIES! You've experienced the snapback effect of willpower.

In one fun study, you know the ones where they ask participants not to think of a polar bear for five minutes, they found that the people who burned through mental energy in the first five minutes were still more likely to think of polar bears in the time after they were no longer trying to control their thoughts.

Forcing yourself into a habit also violates our guiding principles of compassion and self-love. You're in conflict with yourself when you're forcing yourself to act and behave in a certain way. Self-love does not mean letting yourself off the hook completely. That's not acting or caring for your best interests. A child may want to brush their teeth with chocolate milk and eat nothing but chicken nuggets, but a caring parent will ensure they eat their vegetables, learn manners, and get a basic education to give them the best shot.

ENVIRONMENTAL CHANGES

Have you ever noticed how much better you feel in a tidy room versus a messy one? How you'll be less distracted with fewer tabs open? Or how clean bed sheets feel softer and seem to contribute to a better night's sleep?

Our surroundings count more toward our behaviour than we'd all like to admit. It's a comforting story that we're autonomous, independent, free-thinking individuals. This story can help us develop our sense of agency, self-worth, and overall satisfaction.

As we've developed our compassion and empathy, we can often begin to see how others act in their life because of circumstances. We're the same as them. The language you speak, the clothes you wear, what you value—are all heavily influenced by your environment. If water is placed more prominently around canteens than soda, people are much more likely to buy it. The less-healthy version of this is the sweets at the checkout line in petrol stations and grocery stores, making impulse purchases easier.

Our surroundings mold us—sometimes subtly, sometimes obviously. Sometimes it'll quickly influence our behaviour, other times it takes place over the course of years.

As you start to build new habits to bring you toward your ideal life and develop you into your ideal true self, ask how can the environment you're in shape this behaviour for you.

If you want to be more productive, will you be in your living room or home office? If you don't have the luxury of separating the home office and living room, how else can you shape the environment to shape you? Does that mean changing into work clothes for work mode? For example, during the pandemic, what worked for me was sitting on the couch one way for writing and taking calls, and another way for relaxing, reading, and watching TV.

Environment also extends to the people we hang out with and the media we consume. Who would your ideal self associate with more? What would they read, watch, and listen to? I'm not saying change up your whole peer group and stop watching fart comedies. But subtly shift toward the traits you admire, the content you want to watch (curate your Twitter feed, anyone?), and gently allow the better you to be fed by better influences.

Start with one environmental change, get curious about its impact, and revise as you go along.

WHAT REALLY MATTERS? YOU WANT TO SPEND YOUR TIME EARNING, LEARNING, OR RELAXING. — NAVAL RAVIKANT

There are a limited number of actions you can take in a given day. And you do have obligations. I'm not ignoring that. In fact, because of these limits and obligations, you want to focus on what habits will give you the most bang for your buck. When it comes to habits, investing in your health has the greatest return on investment and the best ability to compound. The healthier you are, the more energy you'll have, and the more energy you can put into the other areas of your life. As Confucius says, a healthy man wants a thousand things, a sick man only wants one.

SLEEP

Lack of sleep impacts everything else, it clouds our brain, leads us to be more reactive and hampers our metabolism. We all know how good we feel after a good night's sleep as well too. How tasks become easier, how problems that seemed so insurmountable at night don't look so daunting in the morning light. Also, when you get enough sleep, you don't crave sugar as much, and your body processes it better. So, start with sleep.

A simple suggestion is to start increasing the quantity of sleep you get. If you go to bed around midnight, don't try suddenly going to bed at ten p.m. You'll just stare at the ceiling, and that'll be no use. Instead make the commitment to going to bed before midnight for a week. Taking the example from above of just five more minutes earlier to bedis a great start that will yield big results. The quality of your sleep can be improved by adjusting the room temperature, making the room as dark as possible, avoiding overhead and bright lights in the hours leading up to bed, etc. You don't need to change all of these at once. If you want to dig into sleep, all its benefits, and all the implications of poor-quality sleep, read *Why We Sleep* by Matthew Walker.

EATING

If there's chocolate, sweets, or crisps in the house, you're going to eat them. Clearing out the fridge can be a way of improving your nutritional environment for you. Or you could look at stupidly small habits. Can you drink one glass of water every morning or evening? Could you eat one less chocolate bar a week or drink one less can of Coca-Cola a week? (Not a day, just one a week.)

Yeah, one burger, one cookie, one sugar in your tea doesn't do much. Every day over fifty to seventy years does. Ditto with the glass of water, the side salad, the protein bar, etc. Most diet plans fail because they are too restrictive. The key is, you're not forcing a complete overhaul of your eating habits but implementing subtle shifts that compound.

MOVEMENT

Your body feels better when you move, and your mind will feel better too. In fact, you'll often hear people say they need their daily exercise to feel good. While this isn't the healthiest story we can tell ourselves, it highlights how much of a mood booster it can be.

As someone who owns a Cross-Fit gym, I used to be all about the high intensity, push yourself as hard as you can as often as you can mentality. High intensity has its place, of course. But if you're not used to getting out of breath and feeling sore occasionally, it's not going to be a rewarding experience and encourage you to go again.

What's the least amount of movement you can do each day that you know you can do? Can you take the stairs instead of the elevator once a day? Can you stretch for one minute each day? That might seem like it's not enough, but ask any physical therapist about compliance rates and they'll tell you how little their clients actually follow through consistently on their rehab homework. Think minimum effective dose instead of maximum non-lethal dose.

There are leading indicators and lagging indicators. Going to bed earlier, lifting some weights, eating your greens are all leading indicators. They're actions you can take and tick the box to say you're done. Lagging indicators are the results you want—the increased energy, the bigger muscles, the thinner waistline.

They're all the physical activities that you'll benefit from improving daily, and they'll make a huge difference to your overall energy. For health and fulfilment, two other areas are super important to do deliberately.

CONNECTION

The number one prediction of lifelong health is the depth of our relationships. Intimate, trusting, relationships are what we all need.

We build this through daily, deliberate connection. Scheduling time to connect with people who matter—either arranging your walks with them, talking on the phone, setting aside five minutes when you come home to truly connect, or having a phone-free dinner conversation are all ways in which you build intimacy over time.

If this feels too contrived and not spontaneous or natural enough, remember that the idea that deep, meaningful, and intimate conversations just happen between the right people is more Hallmark movie than scientific fact. The Gottman Institute, which can predict with ridiculous accuracy whether couples stay together or break up, has a short daily-ish podcast (three to five minutes in length), which offers tips on deliberate actions to strengthen your relationships.

You also have the option of genuinely connecting via text these days, if you take the time. Yes, memes and GIFs are a fantastic way to bring a smile to someone's face, and if I could use them exclusively, I probably would!

If you're looking for an immediate, actionable step, next time you're asked how you are, honestly share an answer. What are you feeling? What are you grateful for? What are you working on right now? Like the glass of water, the daily steps, and the extra sleep time, these little actions of vulnerability add up to powerful and reliable connection over time.

What we've been doing up until this point is really connecting with and loving ourselves. In doing so, we're better able to be present with those who matter, express our needs, and have the mental/emotional energy to hold space for them (while also getting our own needs met).

MEANINGFUL ENDEAVOURS

Finally, you need purpose in your life. Apparently, the number one killer in old age is retirement. Having nothing to do can lead to having no purpose and seeming that there's no value and reason to keep going.

Yes, that's an extreme way of looking at it. Most of you reading this probably aren't close to retirement age, so it's not worth considering yet. Having purpose to your day, your life, and everything you do gives your life meaning. **And you get to decide what's meaningful.**

If you're approaching daily tasks as obligations that are taking you away from what you want to do, they're going to drain you and deflate you. If they're contributing to something, while they still might take energy, it's a much different feeling. For example: work stops being just something to get through; it's a means of providing security for your family's future.

As you inject meaning into your daily tasks (they won't just magically have meaning), you will supercharge your agency. And we've been working on this with our daily intentions by asking, "What meaningful thing can I do today?" You can also ask, "What meaning can I bring to this activity?" Even laundry and cleaning the dishes can take on meaning.

"What actions help me feel fulfilled, proud of myself, and give me happiness?" Most of your life satisfaction comes not from the end goal but from a sense of progress. So, what are you capable of making progress toward today?

WHAT HABITS SUPPORT MY PRIORITIES?

You take care of yourself so you can take care of your priorities. This is why I spoke about health habits first. Make sure you charge yourself up as often as you charge your phone's battery. You cannot be an afterthought to all your responsibilities. Your mental health and peace of mind can't be a "nice to have" after you've taken care of your daily obligations and looked after everyone else.

Otherwise, you're just running yourself down, and this will make things worse. Maybe you'll snap at someone, maybe you'll take two hours to complete a simple task, maybe you'll just feel depleted, drained, and depressed at the end of the day.

Topping yourself up as a priority isn't selfish. Things are only selfish if you knowingly ignore the needs of those you care about. Topping yourself up ensures you and everyone who relies on you gets your very best.

Now it's time to go through your priority list and ask what daily, weekly, or monthly habits will sustain and develop them.

For your family, how often do you need to see them? What activities are better scheduled so they don't get pushed aside by seemingly more urgent demands on our time? Do you need two date nights a week with your spouse, or is a monthly one good enough? Could you benefit from a six-second kiss each morning to keep the relationship going? (Hat tip to The Gottman Institute!)

Of course, sometimes emergencies are going to happen and your priorities might shift temporarily. But if you start proactively investing in what's important to you, you're more in control of their growth than simply reacting to whatever is screaming loudest. This is the key difference.

Decide what's truly important.

Create systems to give them the attention they deserve.

Allow the small habits to compound into the results you want.

Written out, it seems like it's sequential: take care of yourself, then take care of your priorities. It's why books and blog articles espousing the benefits of morning routines are so popular. But it doesn't have to be one, then the other. It can be a positive feedback loop of moving the needle forward on your health and your priorities. By proactively setting your environment and daily habits, you continuously shift away from meaningless and unfulfilling daily actions taking over.

HABIT STACKING

You've actually been developing your ability to habit stack since we started this program! We stacked our new morning and evening self-care habits to coffee and brushing our teeth. We put the new habit on top of the existing habit to make it easier to do. That's all habit stacking really is.

Estimates vary wildly on how much of our day is driven by routine habits. Some say forty percent—others say as high as ninety-five! As autonomous as we like to think we are, there's a lot we do out of habit. This isn't an argument to give up and decide that your life is predetermined and there's nothing you can do about it. It's more an acknowledgment that our routines can be optimised so we don't have to put an excessive amount of conscious effort into creating our perfect life.

Habit stacking is a form of implementation intentions: "When this happens, I'll do this." It's setting up a rule ahead of time to steer your behaviour toward the actions you know will pay off favourably. For example:

- When I get home from work, I'll change into my running shoes.
- When it's Wednesday morning, I'll mop the floor.
- When I sit down, I'll read one page before going on my phone.
- When I feel hungry, I'll eat some nuts first before getting a chocolate bar.

Implementation intentions are also very useful for when we fall off the wagon, and we'll return to those in a little bit.

You Can't Talk About Habits Without Referencing James Clear—It's The Law

James Clear wrote the book on habits, literally. *Atomic Habits* lists four main components for getting habits to stick.

Make It Easy: It's easier to spend one minute meditating than one hour. It's easier to clean one cup than the entire house. It's easier to read one page of a book than an entire chapter.

Make It Attractive: Tasty pan-fried vegetables with spice is a lot more appetising than boiled, flavourless greens. The book you enjoy is better than some boring tome.

Make It Obvious: Putting your book on the coffee table makes it obvious it's time to read. Same with your journal or your workout gear.

Make It Rewarding: A pat on the back is one way to make the not-immediately-rewarding tasks more rewarding, enticing you to repeat the behaviour enough times to see results.

What's often forgotten from James Clear's advice is that he says to first decide the person you want to be, and then start voting for that person with your daily actions. This is why we spent so much time determining our identity, values, and priorities before looking at our physical habits.

Let me say it again for the people in the back: There is no rush!

Life is more like a motorway than a racetrack. On a racetrack, we're all starting at the same time, from the same position, with the same objective. So, yes, the comparison matters. On the freeway, we're all coming from different places, traveling in different cars, and headed to different destinations for different reasons.

PREPARING FOR CHALLENGES AND SLIPUPS

Spoiler alert: You're going to mess up. You're going to fumble, be imperfect, and have "failures" along the way when you try to change your habits. The biggest habit mistakes are taking on too much and setting unrealistic expectations of when you'll see a return in the effort invested.

A good few years ago, I had a friend who owned a gym ask me to take an outside look at the place and help him get on track to where he wanted to be. After a chat and a tour, we saw that a lot of little things had slipped leading to an overall messy, chaotic place. I suggested he spend the next week keeping the cubby rack for bags and shoes completely clean, and nothing else. He wanted to do more, so he decided to try to clean the whole gym, spotless, every day. And on top of that, he set new demanding targets on his staff.

Unsurprisingly, when I came back about two months later, the place was in worse disarray than before. He'd asked too much of himself and others in too short a space of time.

Counterintuitive advice, of which this book is full, is—instead of thinking how quickly you can reach your goal, or how much you can do, what about asking what's the least amount of progress you could make today? What's the slowest way to reach your goal?

Secondly, plan for your mulligans. This is the second use of an implementation intention, "When I fall off, this is what I'll do . . ."

When top sports performers practice visualisation, the ones who picture everything going perfectly don't perform as well as the ones who picture things going sideways *and then mentally rehearse how they'd recover from them.*

The important thing is not to be naive and picture everything going flawlessly, or plan for absolute disaster, but rather plan for how you will be okay even if things don't go perfectly. What you'll do when the inevitable setbacks occur. This reaffirms your reassurance!

Dips are going to happen. Being blindsided by them doesn't have to happen.

I actually use this when I hit an inevitable dip in life. When I notice a dip in mood, I focus on my daily Mindset routines, caring self-talk, and look at sleep, nutrition, and movement (especially when I don't want to) to guide me until things start to look up.

BAD BEHAVIOURS

For a start, I think you're telling yourself an unhelpful story when you use the term "bad behaviours." It's not too far of a slip from pinpointing the bad behaviour to guilt and shame. And we all know how a shame spiral goes!

Very often, we can be tempted to try to overcome these bad behaviours through sheer force of will. How's that worked out? One reason why it doesn't work out is because those "bad" behaviours are satisfying some need. So, when you try to stop the bad behaviour, the need that isn't met still claws away at you until you break.

Ask yourself:

What is this behaviour soothing? Is it overwhelm at an emotion? Or boredom eating? Heck when we were younger, we got sweets when we were sick. So, sweets are soothing to me.

What are they attempting to protect you from? Are you checking your phone to avoid difficult work, which can bring up a sense of unworthiness? (He notices this as he keeps going back to his phone instead of typing this.) Are you avoiding it because you don't believe you have the energy or ability right now?

What's another way to satisfy this need?

How can I be compassionate? Can I use caring self-talk to soothe myself instead of engaging in behaviours that go against who I want to be? "Shut up and get to work" hasn't worked!

HOW OFTEN SHOULD I REVIEW MY HABITS?

There is no right or wrong way to improve your habits, so please take the pressure of perfection off yourself. Some say it takes twenty-one days to embed a habit—others sixty-six! I guess the difference in results is how big the habit is and how much conscious effort is required for it to become second nature. Get curious as to what works for you, what's the right level of exertion versus automation. To give you a framework:

Daily: Did I live up to expectations? If you were repeating the day, what tiny change would you make?

Weekly: What new thing would I like to try differently?

Monthly: What's my focus, what area—relationships, career, health, home life, environment?

Quarterly: Are my habits in line with my identity, values, and priorities?

Yearly: Are these still my priorities?

As you become more self-reflective, you'll be more aware of your actions as you're doing them and not just your thoughts while you're on the cushion. Knowing that, you can lovingly ask yourself, "Is this in line with my best interests?" If it's not, ask yourself, "What need is this satisfying?" and look for a better way to soothe your needs.

There are so many circumstances out of our control and factors that play a part in how our lives shape up. But to the extent that our habits are in control, use this question as a guiding principle: Does this behaviour help me become the type of person I want to be?

Colm O'Reilly

SUSTAINABLE COMMUNICATION

Finally, we're at the point where we are ready to invite the cooperation of others into our peace of mind. Because, really, your needs and the needs of others are the one and the same.

Humans are a cooperative species, but the more stressed we are the more combative and antagonistic we'll become. We need other people. We need them to help us. More importantly, and something we often forget, is we want them to want to help us.

Sustainable, or Nonviolent Communication (NVC), as its creator Marshall Rosenberg initially called it, is a style of talking that expresses our needs clearly and invites cooperation instead of resentment in our listener. At its heart is a genuine attempt to clearly understand others and be clearly understood ourselves.

We needed to start with you so you could get clear and tune into your thoughts, feelings, needs, and wants. If you're a mess in your head, and you communicate in a messy way to someone who's also a mess in their head, unable to clearly hear and understand you, how well do you think it's going to go?

As we get clearer in our heads, expressing this to other people not only helps us transmit the thoughts, feelings, and requests we have more precisely, but we also understand ourselves better.

You may notice a lot of commonalities between breaking down the stories in our head and how we'll communicate using NVC. That was deliberate. How you talk to others is a reflection of how you talk to yourself, and let's face it, you talk to yourself all day! Now we're ready to take these improvements into your relationships.

This style of cooperative communication has four steps—data, feelings, needs, and requests. Treat learning this style of speaking the way you would approach learning a foreign language, because for most of us, it will sound clunky at first! I spent six years learning French in school and still could barely communicate with anyone when I took a trip to Paris. It takes time, it's okay to stumble your way forward, and as long as you have a kind, compassionate intention, you'll get it. Each new sentence is a chance to improve your relationships.

DATA, NOT JUDGMENTS

The first stage in cooperative communication is to practice speaking only in observable facts, not judgments. The simple heuristic is never to use "You are . . ." in a moralistic way. "You are lazy," "You don't care about me," "You're always talking," "You never listen," etc.

"You never listen" isn't true anyway, as I'm sure they listened at least once.

When someone hears a sentence starting with "you," instantly we've gotten their back up and put them on the defensive. Even if you're completely right, the response isn't going to be receptive to any ideas you have.

"When I was telling you about my day, I noticed you checked your phone a couple of times," is a data point, or as accurate as we can be. It's worthwhile remembering that as infants we reasoned the world was there for us, and getting our needs met was others' responsibility. From there, it's not too much of a logical jump to also believe that others are the cause of our suffering. Particularly when in a heightened state, we'll default to believe that the cause and solution to our suffering is someone else.

People may be the trigger but not the cause of our emotions. The trigger can be a word or an action. The cause is our interpretation, filtered through memory, judgment, simple misunderstanding, tiredness, and other factors that lead to our reaction. Accepting this is tough! Ultimately, though, it's liberating.

Judgments also serve to separate us. Not only from each other, but from ourselves. Once you've made a judgment, you're closed off to connection with other people and closed off from a curious state of mind.

We judge in a heartbeat. And we judge in the areas where we're prone to shame as well. Judgment is a protection mechanism against openness and vulnerability. It's our way of armouring up. Our scared brains don't realise that armouring up is what's keeping us from the true safety of connection with others.

For example, "You're inconsiderate" is an easy judgement to throw out. The data may be that your request for a date night was rejected (for whatever reason) and the underlying fear is that you aren't worthy or deserving of affection. To guard against processing that belief and the emotions associated with it, you throw out the judgment "you're inconsiderate."

To begin practicing, replace "you are" sentences with, "When I saw this behaviour, this is what I thought . . ." Simply rephrasing judgments into observations will change not only how emotionally reactive you are to events, because by reframing you're challenging your perspective, but it will also invite more dialogue from whoever you're speaking to.

NOBODY MADE YOU FEEL ANYTHING

BETWEEN STIMULUS AND RESPONSE THERE IS A SPACE. IN THAT SPACE IS THE POWER TO CHOOSE OUR RESPONSE. IN THAT SPACE LIES OUR GROWTH AND OUR FREEDOM. —VIKTOR FRANKL

If you could change one part of the way you speak that would help you develop agency and take you away from a victim mentality, it would be to eliminate the phrase "made me." Recall from an earlier section, nobody made you angry, sad, happy, or do anything.

The aim, the goal, the need! is to take full ownership and responsibility for your feelings. Our feelings are ours. And while others may trigger them, we ourselves are the cause of them.

Yes, it's incredibly scary to have to take complete responsibility for our emotions. It can even seem completely unfair. Others are acting like jerks and yet you've got to regulate yourself. They're getting away with their behaviour and not even caring about you.[11] Nobody is "getting away with" anything. While we mightn't be able to see the toll they're paying, they are paying it. Maybe suffering from childhood traumas is the reason they're constantly acting out. Maybe it's loneliness due to their behaviour. Maybe it's the shame of who they are and how they act, or the fear of retribution and a constant need to look over their shoulder. It could even be the hidden cost they don't even know their behaviour is causing them.

Back to us, though. If we can push past the "unfairness" of responsibility for our emotions, it's incredibly liberating and empowering. That's the benefit to us. We're no longer giving away our power.

At this stage, we've spent some time understanding our feelings and the needs underneath them. We started with a daily practice of tuning into them each morning. This took time and was in a calmer, slower setting. Now, the next skill to develop is bringing it into live, dynamic conversation with the people we're interacting with.

"*When this happened, I feel X because I need Y.*"

"*I noticed you did this, it seems to me because of <motive> and I have the feeling X.*"

"You made me," is blaming language. When we think we're being blamed, we instantly become defensive. We close off to listening because

11   According to the story you're telling yourself! ;)

we're busy mentally forming our defence or caught up in an emotional reaction to protect ourselves. By dropping blame, we can invite more curiosity and empathy in the listener.

This way, we don't need the other person to be skilled in NVC, as we'll be using non-triggering language. Yes, it's more work on our part, but it's only more work initially. We gain back the time and effort it takes to be more verbose at the start of the conversation in the time we save by not correcting misunderstandings and de-escalating reactions.

NEEDS & REQUESTS

We have lots of things we'd like people to do and ways for them to behave. We want them to do and say things that will get our needs met, but really, we want them to willingly do these things. We don't want them to begrudgingly help us out or do us a favour only for them to resent us until we've repaid it. This is where requests come into play.

A **demand** is different from a request in that it carries a threat of punishment. *"If you don't fulfill my demand, I'm gonna act out or treat you differently to punish you, and you'll wish you did."* A **request** doesn't carry this implied threat.

Now, that's not to say you could request someone to stop hitting you or any other form of abuse, to use an extreme example. You're still allowed to change the relationship to make sure your needs for safety and significance are met. You can lovingly end any relationship that is no longer getting your needs met.

There's a difference between consequences and punishment. You have needs, say, the need for companionship. You may want your favourite person to give them to you. This is your strategy. If they are unable or unwilling to help you with this need, you can seek companionship elsewhere. You're not punishing them for not being able or willing to do this. You're simply finding another way to take care of your needs.

Adding in the "because" or the reasons for your requests makes them more likely to be granted. We're not going to be manipulative in this. What we are going to do is inform people of the needs behind the requests.

"I'd like to watch a movie with you tonight because I have a need for connection," Is a great example.

There's an informative study about a queue for photocopiers in some university. It's around dissertation time, so there's a long queue. The researchers tried three strategies to see which would be most successful in getting people to cut in line. The first group just asked if they could cut in front and was met with limited success. The second asked if they could jump ahead because they only had a few copies to make and were in a rush. These requests were granted a lot more. And the third simply asked if they could cut ahead because they've copies to make. The exact same reason *everyone* was in the line waiting for the photocopiers! What's amazing is that the results were almost identical in the two "reasoned" groups.

WHAT IF THEY SAY NO?

If they say no, we can attempt to understand their needs and see if there's a solution that gets everyone's needs met. Ideally, together. But if not, at least everyone's needs are accounted for and every attempt to accommodate them is made.

"It seems like you have a need to be alone tonight to recharge your batteries, and I have a need for connection. Would it be possible to have a phone call instead? Or arrange some time to hang out tomorrow so we could both get what we need?"

As we begin to ask these questions, we're taking into account everyone's needs. No longer are you asking another to sacrifice for you, nor are you subjugating your needs to appease someone else. Win–lose or lose–win is unsustainable and unworkable.

What's more, you're no longer demanding that there's only one person or one strategy to get your needs met. This isn't a way of compromising that everyone thinks they've lost out, aren't fully happy, and end up with resentment. You can communicate, really communicate, knowing that, if one strategy isn't going to completely satisfy your needs, you have other options on the table too.

Reminder that a strategy is a means of getting a fundamental need met. If it's only partially getting your needs met, you're free to seek additional strategies on top of the agreement you're reaching with your discourse partner.

CONVOLUTED?

I'm not going to lie, this doesn't flow as naturally as most of us speak. Like learning another language, it's going to be clunky initially and you'll probably feel self-conscious as you attempt to use the principles.

Every thought pattern in your head has been a learned pattern. You don't think in Cantonese, you think in English. How you form sentences (both in your head and out loud) is a learned behaviour and only seems "natural" now because of repetition. The same will become true of separating out observable facts, judgments, feelings, needs, and requests. It's no more convoluted than any other way of speaking you've learned so far. The difference is this is a conscious attempt at cooperation.

Manipulative? Chris Voss, former FBI hostage negotiator and author of "Never Split The Difference: Negotiating As If Your Life Depended On It", said it's manipulative when you're trying to get what you want at the expense of another. The difference between that and influence is that influence is trying to help someone overcome a mental block and ensuring everyone's needs are met.

DOES THAT MAKE SENSE?

How often have we said, "Does that make sense?" or "Do you understand me?" or "Am I making myself clear?" only to get a nod of agreement? For our part, how many times have we said yes without really agreeing with them or even understanding them? Or you say "yeah," but you really haven't a clue what the agreement is. Or, even worse, you both think you've agreed but you've agreed on very different things!

You ask this question because usually because you're short on time. You don't want to be patronising. Yet, by saving time with this question, we end up with a lot of misunderstandings.

Instead, you're better served by asking them to repeat back to you what they heard so you both can reach a consensus.

"Hey, I want to make sure I was clear, can you let me know what you heard me say?" is a non-threatening way of seeking clarification. "Hey, dumbass, I want to make sure your dumb ass was listening, repeat back what you heard!" is a less cooperative style of communication.

LISTENING EMPATHETICALLY

A friend confided in me that early on in his career he'd listen so intently that he'd hear a pin drop. He could recall in his mind every single word that was said. The problem was that he never let the other person know he'd heard everything.

Too often we listen to respond, awaiting our turn to speak. Or we get triggered and feel the compelling desire to react and defend ourselves.

It's worth a small detour to investigate why we do this. Simply put, in the moment, we can sense a threat. Our human need for connection is so important that in a split second we can forget that we're capable of being the source of all our approval, security, and control. We can fulfill our needs. Easy to tell yourself that when you're sitting on the cushion in your formal meditation practice. Much, much harder when you're in the real world. We'll talk about what to do when someone triggers you in a little bit. For now, understand that making someone the source of your needs is largely why we listen to respond or react. (Or even don't bother listening because what we've got to say is way more important anyway!)

You're not a failure if you notice how often you're uninterested in what someone else is saying because your current issues are so overwhelming that you can't focus on another. You're a human. And it's okay to be in a threatened state.[12]

Simply begin by noticing every time you're not really listening. At first, this will be all the flipping time. Training yourself to patiently wait your turn to speak is a skill—and one you absolutely get better at the more you practice.

Much like when we started practicing kindness—the idea that if we have enough we won't be so needy and will naturally look to share the wealth amongst our nearest and dearest—the same is true with empathetic listening. As you practice it more, the less you'll be driven by the overwhelming urge to have someone listen to you. This isn't to say that it's not important to have someone who's able to extend back to you the same compassion and empathy, merely that the uncomfortable sensation of needing to be heard will lessen.

As you listen more, you'll also notice that your thoughts will clarify further. It's not a zero-sum game where if you give the other person all the space they need to be heard you'll lose out. (See, notice how a fear-based rationale impacts your connection with others and yourself? It's sneaky, isn't it?)

---

12 The more we remind ourselves that most of us, most of the time, are in a threatened state, the less likely we'll be in a threatened state and triggered by others.

HOW DO YOU LISTEN EMPATHETICALLY THEN?

LISTEN TO UNDERSTAND

As cliché as it is, the attitude of curiosity is the first prerequisite to be able to listen empathetically. If you already know what they're going to say or where they're coming from, it's a sign you've already formed a judgment and you've closed yourself off to learning. Initially, you'll most likely have to practice this in less-than-heated conversations. But the urge to absolutely need to get your point across to them is a great sign you'd be better served by listening more.

If you want a purely selfish reason, the closer you listen to their assumptions, judgments, and conclusions, the more accurately you'll be able to pinpoint your rebuttal and help them see the flaw in their argument and how right you actually are!

REFLECT

As you listen to your fellow human, the first stage to active, empathetic listening is to reflect back what you heard. This step alone, without going into any more detail, will help them feel "felt" and also provide the perfect opportunity to gain an understanding.

You can either paraphrase by repeating back in your own words, or parrot exactly what they said verbatim. No one ever thinks this is weird if you're genuinely trying to understand. If you feel self-conscious or uncomfortable, start by saying, "Just so I understand what you said," or "What I heard you say," as a preface.

Ideally. you'd wait until they stop talking, but you might be reaching your capacity to take in new information, so it's okay to interrupt them to cache the data they've transferred. "Hey, I want to hear everything you have to say, can I interrupt just to make sure I've gotten everything so far?"

If they interrupt your summary of their points, that's great! They believe they're being listened to, so they're already softened and more agreeable. At any point, once you've repeated back the phrase, ask them if there's anything you missed or anything else they'd like to add.

BUT WHAT IF SOMETHING TRIGGERS YOU?

What if they say something that's patently untrue or is a hot topic for you? What if they attack your values and morals, or take an opposite stance on a political hotbed issue for you?

You probably know now from performative Twitter spats and TV soundbites that shouting back louder won't work. When has someone telling you you're wrong or an idiot for being wrong ever changed your mind? More likely, it's led to you digging your heels in even more.

Three strategies come to mind here. The first is to get curious and notice what's going on inside you. How quickly can you become aware of your reactions and your triggers? From there, you move to a place of welcoming the emotions and getting curious about what's underneath them. It's doable, it just takes practice, and with time you'll be able to stay curious most of the time, even with hot triggers.

Is your "need" to be right threatening your need for security, or connection, or significance? How can you be curious about what's going on inside you when you get triggered and emotional? How can you treat yourself compassionately instead of shutting down the emotion or lashing out because of it?

The second is to ask questions with the aim of understanding what was said to you and what they meant rather than assuming the worst. Was it an insult? What about their reasoning? What's going on with their worldview and assumptions that would lead them to say this? Repeating back here in a curious tone can help you understand their motive. There's a difference between compassionate inquiry and "What the f*ck did you just say?"

Finally, you can interrupt and ask for a time-out, noting that you're getting triggered and unable to really listen to them right now. Press pause and get space so you can come down from your heightened state. You can reassure them you will return to the conversation and be better able to hear them out.

VALIDATE

I NEVER ALLOW MYSELF TO HAVE AN OPINION ON ANYTHING THAT I DON'T KNOW THE OTHER SIDE'S ARGUMENT BETTER THAN THEY DO.
— CHARLIE MUNGER

Justify their reasoning by recreating it for them. You don't have to agree. In fact, especially if what they said is complete bull, this is not the time to tell them they're full of it (even if they really are)!

Follow the steps so you understand their point of view, not so you can highlight where their logic falls. You'll get that chance after you've helped them by listening and understanding where they're coming from *and* you've asked permission to share your point of view. It helps to know their point of view from start to finish. The better you understand their argument the easier it will be to deconstruct. Of course, we're doing it from a place of caring and compassion, not manipulation.

I heard a podcast with Shannon Foley Martinez, a former violent white supremacist who now devotes her time helping people avoid the same fate, recently where she, being in favor of gun control, discussed gun ownership with someone who was adamantly pro Second Amendment. Very easy to get caught up in right versus wrong, me versus you in this contentious debate. Shannon took the approach to understand why her fellow human took an opposite stance to her. They both wanted to keep their families safe. Both had the same underlying motive. Knowing this, they could have a more compassionate discourse as they'd found common ground. Now, Ms. Foley Martinez didn't join the NRA, nor did her compatriot surrender her Glock. The attempt at understanding led to greater communication instead of disconnection.

I've deliberately picked a contentious issue to illustrate that the aim is to understand. The more we understand, especially if we disagree, the less we'll be worked up and the easier it'll be to find a solution that gets both parties' needs met.

ACTUAL EMPATHY

Empathy is "feeling with" someone. Once you've paraphrased and reconstructed their argument, you can presumptively name their emotion for them, and need.

"Because you didn't get a text from me, you thought I didn't care, and this has you feeling sad and needing reassurance?"

If you phrase it as a question, and genuinely give a damn enough to empathise, it really doesn't matter if you get the emotion or the need wrong. As you've no doubt discovered with yourself, you aren't a hundred percent certain what you're thinking and feeling most of the time. It's highly unlikely they are either. As psychologist and expert on codependance, childhood trauma and emotional development Pia Mellod said, "Most of us can't figure out why we are feeling the way we do, much less why others feel the way they do." By phrasing the question and parsing out their emotional reasoning, you've already helped them get closer to the truth.

When I was first learning this, I asked my then-girlfriend what she was feeling. She replied she was "feeling that . . ." to which I retorted, "That's not a f*cking feeling!" Needless to say, this didn't go well! Luckily, I've learned to refine how I check in with people's emotions!

TELL ME MORE

You can always ask for more. More clarification, more detail, or anything else that wasn't already said.

So often, just doing this negates your need to defend your position or present your argument. But if you do want to share now, your partner is more primed to listen. Particularly if you ask first. "I'd like to share what's going on with me now." "I'd like to share how I see it, is that okay?"

"Let me tell you what really happened, you dumbass!" isn't an advisable strategy here.

Finally, then you can speak! But be prepared to be misunderstood. If and when that's the case, you can always repeat back, "You heard me say X? Let me clarify, I meant Y . . ."

Written out like this it can seem very laborious and tedious to go through all the clarification and "waste" time really understanding the other person (particularly when you know they're wrong and you have to tell them the truth). This is the upfront investment that prevents so many squabbles long term.

Ultimately, all this boils down to is a simple strategy to enable clear, compassionate, and curious conversation, coming from a sincere desire to be understood and to understand each other so that everyone can win. A good question to ask yourself as you phrase your words is "is this likely to invite cooperation or resentment?" Holding that intention will help you as we all muddle our way through building better relationships.

WHEN YOU WAKE UP IN THE MORNING, TELL YOURSELF: THE PEOPLE I DEAL WITH TODAY WILL BE MEDDLING, UNGRATEFUL, ARROGANT, DISHONEST, JEALOUS AND SURLY. THEY ARE LIKE THIS BECAUSE THEY CAN'T TELL GOOD FROM EVIL. BUT I HAVE SEEN THE BEAUTY OF GOOD, AND THE UGLINESS OF EVIL, AND HAVE REC-OGNIZED THAT THE WRONGDOER HAS A NATURE RELATED TO MY OWN - NOT OF THE SAME BLOOD AND BIRTH, BUT THE SAME MIND, AND POSSESSING A SHARE OF THE DIVINE. AND SO NONE OF THEM CAN HURT ME. NO ONE CAN IMPLICATE ME IN UGLINESS. NOR CAN I FEEL ANGRY AT MY RELATIVE, OR HATE HIM. WE WERE BORN TO WORK TOGETHER LIKE FEET, HANDS AND EYES, LIKE THE TWO ROWS OF TEETH, UPPER AND LOWER. TO OBSTRUCT EACH OTHER IS UNNATURAL. TO FEEL ANGER AT SOMEONE, TO TURN YOUR BACK ON HIM: THESE ARE UNNATURAL.
- MARCUS AURELIUS, MEDITATIONS

Colm O'Reilly

GOING DEEP

LEANING INTO YOUR PAIN

Inner work cannot be just thinking happy thoughts and clearing your mind. You can't use "self-care" as an excuse to avoid uncomfortable truths. This is called spiritual bypassing. Denying your pain and your trauma, or your destructive thoughts or behaviours will only lead to them bleeding out in some way, shape, or form.

To paraphrase Tim Ferriss, by not dealing with it, you are dealing with it. The dark side of you, your demons, your "bad" behaviour, is still there and still influencing you regardless of whether you look at it or not. The overdrawn bank account you're not checking is still accruing interest. Or a tumor that you refuse to get checked out is still growing.

Apologies for the potential scare tactics here; I simply want to highlight how important it is that we lean into what's not working instead of trying to drown it out with happy thoughts.

Huge amounts of clarity, curiosity, and compassion are needed to not react or buy into your fears and destructive beliefs. (I'm defining "destructive beliefs" as anything you think about yourself or about the world that is a cause of suffering.) With clarity, you can help pinpoint exactly what the destructive belief is. With curiosity, you can investigate how it shows up, where it came from, and what purpose it's serving. Compassion helps you to understand you're not alone in being less than perfect.

Tsultrim Altrione in *Feeding Your Demons* offers a Buddhist perspective on dealing with this. Literally sit down and have a conversation with your demons, your internal beliefs. Set up two cushions, sit down, and visualise your demon in as much detail as you can. Next up, ask them what they want from you and what they need, then swap places. As the demon, answer what you want (for example, stop putting yourself out there) and what you need (to feel secure and safe). Then, back as you, you give them what they need until they're satisfied. Literally imagine yourself dissolving into a ball of light or energy and feeding the demon what they need.

The crux of her work, as I understand it, is that your demons are acting tough to protect themselves, and they need warmth and affection. They need caring. By fighting them or ignoring them they'll only grow bigger, uglier, and more vicious. But by witnessing them and feeding them, they shrink away, and you can heal them.

Richard Swartz, founder of Internal Family Systems, offers a more Western psychological approach to the same idea. Our demons, to Swartz, are our "protectors," defending the scared and wounded parts of us—our "exiles." His approach is to find your Self (capital-S), the part of you that is always centred, calm, curious, etc. From here, you can talk to your protector and ask them what they're defending. Once they're listened to and understood, not argued with, we can ask them what they'd need to let us take control and what they'd do instead of defending us.

There's more to both approaches than I've surmised here, and I'd highly encourage learning from them directly. The key takeaway is to look upon your dark side as someone scared and in need of reassurance, not some evil enemy that needs to be defeated.

It can be really scary to turn toward them, but is it any scarier than living in the fear that the demons will take control and ruin everything for you? The courage of turning toward them, at your speed, in your time, will repay itself in a deeper compassion for yourself and everyone else's struggles. And the benefit of turning toward them is that you no longer have to burn the massive amounts of energy running away from them.

By first building up your awareness, compassion, kindness, and forgiveness you equip yourself with the resources necessary to explore your "bad side" and unresolved pain. When you're ready, wade into those waters at the pace that's right for you.

As you do, remember we're all works in progress, we're all carrying some burdens, and we're all imperfect human beings.

THERAPY?

We all have historical traumas to clear and blind spots in our self-awareness. This is where a coach, therapist, or any nonattached compassionate sounding board helps. In fact, I look forward to the day when people talk about psychotherapists the same way they talk about physiotherapists. No one judges someone when they say they're going to a physio. It's normalised. We don't hide it or feel embarrassed or ashamed when we say we're getting some muscle tightness worked out. But we rarely share the same thing when we're getting help with some mental tightness!

Even the word "psychotherapy" sounds harsh. Let me explain why and how it's beneficial.

Dentists are super important, as they can give our teeth and gums deep cleaning. But we don't rely on dentists to keep our oral health in top shape. We have a daily practice of brushing and flossing. We use both the dentist and our toothbrush with the frequency that's right for us. Sometimes that might be an intense period of visits, and other times it's a couple of months between check-ins. A therapist helps with a periodic deep clean or a specific issue, like an extraction. What's important is you keep up the regular cleaning and flossing daily, which is what we've been building into our practice.

A friend of mine takes care of my dog when I'm away. They're besties. Once, after staying with her, she asked me to leave the long lead for him next time. I was initially confused as he only has one lead. It's one that folds over on itself to make variable lengths, but she'd missed this fact and had it folded to its shortest length. Once she saw the extra clips, she was able to adjust it back to the long lead.

This girl is super intelligent! The point I'm making with the story is that we all have blind spots. Even if we spend all our time observing our inner world, we'll still miss certain things. This is one of the reasons why having an external confidante is so important. They help us adjust our lenses.

Lori Gottlieb, author of the amazing book *Maybe You Should Talk to Someone* explains that therapists give us "wise compassion." If you explain to a friend how your ex was such a jerk, your friend will agree with you, call them the villain, and take your side. While this may be comforting in the moment, you might be missing out on growth and self-reflection. A therapist will be more likely to safely (if not completely comfortably) look at your involvement and what you did to make the relationship play out like it did. With this wise compassion, you are more aware and less likely to repeat the pattern.

While you need to start by looking inward and understanding your thoughts, feelings, and needs, it doesn't mean you have to figure it all out on your own.

We make sense of the world through our discussions with others as much as through our discussions with ourselves. Without investing in gaining clarity on what's going on with us, what's really our issue versus someone else's, clear communication is next to impossible. But clear communication is vital. How often has the surefire thought in your head failed to sustain itself once you've said it out loud? Making the internal jumble coherent to be understood by someone who doesn't have the context (or baggage) can be enough to rid yourself of a delusional or unhelpful viewpoint.

So, ultimately, the more we can have clear, compassionate communication with trusted sources the more likely we'll create a virtuous loop of internal and external discovery/improvement.

Communication with others is vital because, while it's important to take responsibility for the fulfilment of your needs, the strategy will most likely rely on the cooperation of others. You'll need your friends and partner to want to spend time with you, your boss to want to continue employing you, or your customers to continue purchasing your products. Communicating from a place of curiosity and with the aim of everybody winning (getting their needs met) improves everyone's lives, especially yours.

SELF-CARE IS JUST ONE PART OF YOUR LIFE

While you absolutely need to take personal responsibility for your life, you weren't born in a vacuum, and we aren't all on a level playing field. There are legitimate concerns outside of your mind. The aim in this book was and is to give you clear step-by-step instructions on how to mind your mind. Once again, that's not to say that it's all in your head. You need sleep, food, and physical movement daily just for basic health. To try and just focus on your thoughts and feelings is another form of spiritual bypassing—it's ignoring your issues and burying your head in the sand.

So, how would you know if your inner work has drifted into escapism?

If you're waiting until you're free, fixed, healed, or "no longer broken" to take action in a new career, relationship, or living situation, you could be using inner work as an escape or a means of protecting yourself. Ideally, all aspects of your life should support each other, or at least live in harmonious tension. You mightn't totally love your job; but for now, it sustains you financially.

If you're sacrificing other areas of your life to the point where the marginal gains from improved inner peace outweigh the gains from physical health, relationship health, or financial health, you've drifted too far and would benefit from a correction. Let's be clear on this point: You get to decide what fit enough, wealthy enough, productive enough is. If your meditation practice is two hours a day and yet you struggle to pay rent, it's time to rebalance. The same is true if your bank account is bulging but you've no time for your self-care.

I remember a handstand seminar we hosted once at my gym. The instructor pointed out that balance isn't something you get, it's something you're constantly working on. It's an active process. It's a great little analogy for life.

Ultimately, the best indicator of too much introspection and self-care is when the pursuit of inner peace is making you unhappy. This whole thing is a constant process of refinement. There's never going to be the perfect iteration that will allow you to coast your way throughout the rest of your life. As M. Scott Peck points out in *The Road Less Travelled*, you will need to constantly update your map of meaning for the world.

Don't fall into mental escapism. You need other people; you need meaningful pursuits.

That's a given. You also need security. If you're reading this, your physical security from war is probably close to zero for a civilian. Depending on your neighbourhood, your risk of physical violence may be high or low. For most of us, we're living in the least-violent time in history, and from that standpoint, the safest. Where our security threat lies is most likely an economic one. Your shelter and nourishment are dictated by your ability to make money in society. That's important.

As money worries are one of the most common triggers for people's anxieties, we'll address it briefly here as an example of how to mindfully and compassionately approach it.

If we're motivated by fear, it'll lead us to short-term survival thinking. We need an understanding of how to soothe and comfort ourselves, though, otherwise the fear will continue even when we're no longer in danger of bankruptcy or starvation. I don't think anyone would argue that anyone with a billion dollars has enough money, yet we still see billionaires hoard money out of the belief they don't have enough. Clearly, it's not money alone that will solve the fear issue.

It's an extreme example to illustrate the point. Before we reach a healthy financial target, can we act out of compassion (or love, or trust, whatever word resonates best with you) instead of fear?

Can you assure yourself that, right now, in this moment, you're okay? If you're able to read this right now, in this very moment, you're safe. That's not to say you don't need to act to guarantee future safety. Simply that right now, you're okay. And if you're okay in this moment, it's likely you'll be okay in the next moment. This mantra, or gentle coaxing, may be required *a lot* when fear rears its ugly head. As with all our skills, the more we practice it the better we'll become at guiding ourselves.

I can't tell you what exact steps you may need to take to improve your financial security. Or maybe your finances are in order but it's physical fitness, repairing familial relationships, or fulfilling pursuits without risking your safety that you need to improve upon.

What is in your control is micro-steps daily to improve your situation, compassionately taken, and with a trusting attitude. So, when the big challenges or opportunities or leaps of faith come around, you're as prepared as you can be.

Colm O'Reilly

ENOUGH

It's probably one of the greatest acts of self-care (and therefore care to others) to define exactly what is enough to you. Firstly, let's look at "good enough." It took me a long time to realise that a lot of my underlying fears all centred around not being good enough. Not being good enough gave my inner demons plenty of fuel to stop me taking action, beat me down, and ridicule me for my patheticness. What made their power even greater is that the standard of being good enough wasn't defined at all. And you can't hit a target you don't define.

Seth Godin said that quality is whatever meets the standard, i.e., good enough = quality. What does good enough mean when it comes to your education level? For some, it's a pass grade at the undergraduate level; for others, it's Nobel prize levels of academic achievement.

It will take time to clearly define what good enough means for you in the areas that matter in your life. They'll be tied to your unique values and priorities as well. For some, a good enough car is one that works most of the time. For others, it needs to be the latest luxury model. How clean your kitchen and bathroom are can also be defined. I use this example as I know firsthand that not clarifying this can lead to a lot of arguments! Starting out, can you define what's enough coffee each day, or sleep? What's enough time spent on TikTok? What's enough time invested in your education, your leisure, in charitable work and donations, in different relationships?

Equally important in all of this is what level of introspection and self-improvement is enough. At what point are you seeing diminishing returns and costing yourself more than you're getting back?

What is enough to you? It's a weird question, one you may not have ever been asked or deliberately decided to ask yourself.

What's enough money, sex, free time, work time?

What's enough sacrifice, effort, altruism?

Why is this important? If we don't decide what's enough, we've no measuring stick to let us know when it's too much or too little. The trap of "never enough" keeps us suffering when it's no longer a noble struggle.

Laurie Santos in her excellent course, The Science of Well-Being, notes that, regardless of salary, people think 150% of what they currently make will be enough for them and finally make them happy. Of course, this viewpoint was held no matter how often their salary reached 150% of what it previously was.

When we can understand what is enough for ourselves, we can begin to articulate what is enough to others. They won't just know, no matter how close you are. What's enough alone time, fun time, serious time, etc.

Dare to ask and define what's enough as you build increased clarity and compassion.

But, ultimately, the concept of "enough" is important because you will need to tell yourself repeatedly that you are enough. As you are right now, a human being, you're enough. You don't have to do and attain more in order to be valid and accepted.

This concept often gets confused because people will have a sense that they're not enough for something or someone. It's a product of external forces and the dark side of desire. Enough needs to be a self-defined concept, much like we worked on establishing your identity, values, and priorities for yourself.

No, right now, I don't have enough in the bank for a Porsche. There's a subtle but powerful difference between "I don't have enough for X right now," and "I don't have enough." By shortening the first sentence into the second one, we make it about insufficiency, which triggers our survival mechanism. It's absolutely fine to have wants and desires. They can provide important targets for us to make progress toward. But, if we place our happiness on the achievement of them, we've essentially made a deal with ourselves to be unhappy, unfulfilled, and insufficient until they're achieved—i.e., not enough.

Right now, you are enough.

You have enough.

You've done enough. And you'll do enough.

You are enough.

Colm O'Reilly

ACKNOWLEDGMENTS

First of all, I want to thank my clients, who have trusted me to share what I've learned with them, given me feedback, and made my service and this book better.

I want to thank all my good and bad experiences, as they've all led to where I am today.

And most importantly, you, for devoting your time to reading this.

Colm O'Reilly

FURTHER READING

10% Happier by Dan Harris

Already Free by Bruce Trift

Love Yourself Like Your Life Depends on It by Kamal Ravikant

Nonviolent Communication by Marshall B. Rosenberg

Atomic Habits by James Clear

The Almanack of Naval Ravikant by Eric Jorgenson

No Bad Parts by Richard Schwartz

Feelings Wheel

Based on Nonviolent Communication by Marshall Rosenberg, Ph.D. May be duplicated for personal use and for teaching Nonviolent Communication. Graphics and organization of feelings and needs wheels by Bret Stein. artisantf@hotmail.com Revised 1/1/11

Feelings are <u>internal</u> emotions. Words mistaken for emotions, but that are actually thoughts in the form of evaluations and judgments of others, are any words that follow "I feel like ... " or "I feel that ..." or "I feel as if ..." or "I feel you ...", such as:

Abandoned	Attacked	Abused	Betrayed	Blamed	Bullied	Cheated
Coerced	Criticized	Dismissed	Disrespected	Excluded	Ignored	Intimidated
Insulted	Let Down	Manipulated	Misunderstood	Neglected	Put down	Rejected
Unappreciated	Unloved	Unheard	Unwanted	Used	Violated	Wronged

Needs Wheel

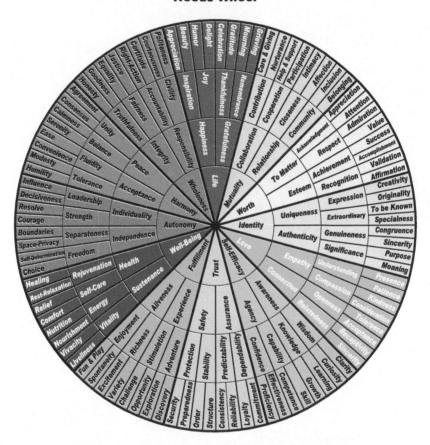

Based on Nonviolent Communication by Marshall Rosenberg, Ph.D. May be duplicated for personal use and for teaching Nonviolent Communication. Graphics and organization of Feelings and Needs Wheels by Bret Stein. artisantf@hotmail.com Revised 1/1/11

Needs are <u>internal</u> values which are important to everyone. Words mistaken for Needs, but that are actually strategies to meet Needs are any <u>external</u> behaviors, such as anything that follows "I need you to ... ":

Comply   Apologize   Validate me   Conform   Respect me   Obey   Give me

Colm O'Reilly

Made in the USA
Las Vegas, NV
21 November 2023